FABRICE HERGOTT

ROUAULT

EDICIONES POLÍGRAFA, S. A.

*We should like to express our gratitude
to Madame Isabelle Rouault and to Madame
Geneviève Nouaille Rouault for their
invaluable assistance in the preparation
of this book.*

© *1991 Ediciones Polígrafa, S. A.*
Balmes, 54 - 08007 BARCELONA (Spain)

Reproduction rights: © ADAGP, Paris

English translation: RICHARD REES

I.S.B.N.: 84-343-0693-X
Dep. Legal: B. 25.221 - 1992 (Printed in Spain)

Photogravure: Reprocolor Llovet, S. A.
Printed by La Polígrafa, S. A.
Parets del Vallès (Barcelona)

CONTENTS

Georges Rouault in his studio, at the age of eighty-two (1953)

GEORGES ROUAULT

Present in major collections, the work of Rouault occupies a clearly differentiated position in contemporary art since it is one of the rare examples in the modern western world of a perfectly realized religious art. To this must be added the personality of this secretive and inscrutable painter who devoted his life entirely to art, a life which became a legend many years before his death, which took place over thirty years ago.

Somewhere between Mark Twain's popular heroes, by virtue of his origins, and the self-imposed demands of Huysmans, by virtue of the scruples he felt in the face of his own works, Rouault appears almost as a character from a XIX-century novel. Nevertheless, he is one of the great names of modern art, a painter difficult to link to the different artistic avant-gardes.

At the turn of the century Rouault was one of the first to follow the most daring paths and persevere in a direction which was at first understood only by a few of his friends. What appeared to be audacious in his paintings prior to the Great War became self-evident thirty or forty years later. Neither a Fauve nor a Cubist, Rouault was never concerned with abstract art. He figured in none of the groups of artists who played a direct avant-garde role; on the contrary, he played this role in private. The widely applied label "expressionist" does not suit him at all; in his painting there is nothing exaggerated, neither smudges of vivid red nor broken lines; nor after his formative period is there anything reminiscent of academicism or tending towards the repetition of a formula. His confidence in observation of nature led him to ignore Surrealism to the same extent that Surrealism ignored him. Indeed, his contribution to modern art is still difficult to evaluate due to the lack of elements of comparison. The masterpieces he produced in the different periods of his artistic development, using constantly renewed media, are isolated crystallizations, difficult to relate to the chronological context of museum events.

In an irrational century, given to entertainment and excess, Rouault's canvases seem to be painted with the pride of the craftsman. His honor consisted in working, in believing that this work was his strength. He liked to quote Poussin's saying that "painting is a mute art."

In order not to perturb their vision of the canvases into which Rouault had concentrated his thought, critics and theorists always placed him in a category apart, where he was happy to remain, partly through timidity but above all to ensure the proper conditions in which to carry out what he had proposed. His work both required and benefited from this isolation. Rouault worked tenaciously to achieve an ideal. As a "peasant tied to the soil of painting," as he liked to define himself, he gave himself body and soul to his canvases and engravings, to attain not glory or material wealth but spiritual satisfaction. Religion provided him with the measure of what he had to do, and he described himself as a "Christian painter."

Rouault admired Cézanne, the man and his work. There can be no doubt that the dominant blues and the monumental composition of his early watercolors owe much to Cézanne's portraits and landscapes of 1890-1900 which were first shown in Paris around 1904. Rouault paid him homage in the form of a fictitious monologue in his first published text, dated 1910 and titled *Noli me tangere* (Touch me not). The title alludes to an incident that took place near Aix, where the painter and critic Émile Bernard attempted to prevent Cézanne from falling when the latter tripped. Cézanne flew into a rage and protested: "Nobody will touch me... ever, ever!" Rouault related this anecdote, published in 1907 after Cézanne's death, to the words uttered by Christ on the morning of his resurrection, "without wishing to deify the painter." Rouault appropriated the distance Cézanne had established between himself and the world: "I want to die in peace," he writes at the end of his text, "far from the noise and the lies of life. In essence my art, though modest and humble, has not defrauded me; far from disappointing theories, I have managed at certain times to find my corner of paradise lost." When he wrote this, Rouault was not yet forty.

* * *

Georges Rouault was born in May 1871 in a basement in Rue de la Villette, where his mother had taken shelter from the bombardments by the Versailles troops who were then entering Paris. His first weeks of life were marked by the civil war and the terrible reprisals that ensued. He grew up in Belleville, which at that time was a village. Probably his memories of poverty and his observations of misery occupied an essential place in the view he would subsequently have of the world and in the spirit of his paintings. The crepuscular landscapes which abound in his oeuvre, such as in *Slums of the Great Sorrows*, undoubtedly contain much of the climate and the urban scenes of his childhood.

His father was a joiner so preoccupied with the perfection of his work that he could not bear to hear a drawer squeaking or to see anyone mistreating wood. He was a great admirer of Lamennais, that now forgotten thinker who in his writings attempted to reconcile a certain evangelistic spirit with the working-class world of the XIX century. He had his son christened, although he did not bring him up in a religious way.

Rouault's early interest in art came from his maternal grandfather, Champdavoine, who collected prints by Manet, Courbet and Daumier that could be purchased at the antique book stalls dotted along the banks of the

Seine. At the age of five, Rouault drew large faces in chalk on the kitchen floor. Extremely shy in temperament, whenever he had to accompany his mother to visit someone he did not know or disliked, he had to be dragged from under the bed where he had taken refuge.

At the age of fourteen, after the death of his grandfather, he entered a master glazier's studio as an apprentice. Often, at lunchtime, he would remain behind to contemplate the copies of old stained-glass windows among the imitations, using this technique, of the *tableaux vivants* so much in vogue at the time and the staple production of the studio. He went to evening drawing classes at the École des Arts Décoratifs, where some of his first academic studies are still preserved. As he detested "thankless mechanical work," he rejected job proposals made to him and, at the end of 1890, enrolled in the classes of Élie Delaunay, an academic painter, as were all the teachers at the École des Beaux-Arts. Delaunay died just under a year later, but before his death he had taken the trouble to recommend his friend Gustave Moreau as his successor. In 1892, when he took up his post, Moreau was almost seventy years old. His *Oedipus and the Sphinx*, prize winner at the official Salon of 1864, and *Salome Dancing before Herod* (1876) had earned him fame as a painter, although few of his colleagues appreciated his work. "He met with harsh, silent opposition," wrote Rouault in his *Souvenirs intimes*, "both inside and outside the School. What people objected to . . . was his spiritual sense that stood in opposition to naturalism and to a certain official conformism."

Even so, Moreau certainly had his defenders. The writer Huysmans eulogized him in several pages of art criticism, and before that had made him the favorite painter of Des Esseintes, the protagonist of his novel *À rebours*. He also had a considerable number of admirers among the young poets and painters whose sensitivity would enlighten the broad and fecund symbolist movement. Even the terrible Degas, who had dedicated some ferociously ironic words to him, professed a genuine affection for Moreau. Both felt a deep veneration for Ingres and both evoked with the same modesty works by those who were then called the "ancients" or old masters.

Moreau proved to be an incomparable teacher. In reference once again to his master, Rouault wrote: "What considerateness he had, what delicate respect for life and nuances. 'I wish you late success,' he told me. 'An artist who has made a name for himself by the time he is thirty is already lost for certain kinds of art . . . I see you as becoming more and more isolated and solitary: you favor a grave, sober art, religious in its essence.' . . . He tried to awaken our taste, to form it through the constant study of the ancients and of nature, yet without excessive rigor or puritanism. He was the first to arrive at the School and the last to leave. Sometimes he would be seen in the *Cour du Mûrier* or in some corner sketching an ancient motif in his album. As he was leaving, the novices would cling to the tails of his frock coat and plead 'Monsieur Moreau, correct us!' He was younger at heart than most of us. I recall that one day he paused in front of the model and confessed: 'This flesh is admirable against the gray background; how I would love to be able still to paint with you. One thinks one knows, but then realizes that one knows nothing.'"

Unlike most of his colleagues, Moreau obliged his pupils to paint, and was gratified when they did more than simply imitate him. He was highly receptive to all their observations and suggestions, and for him all that was valid was inner feeling. His affinities with Symbolism permitted him to understand personal beliefs and to discover the expression of the individual through his dreams. Twenty years later the young Surrealists were not mistaken: via the highly peculiar atmosphere of his museum, Gustave Moreau would also act as a stimulus for them.

For his pupils, Moreau was not only a model of technique but also a norm of life and a call of attention to the real world. With them he crossed the bridge of the Arts and took them to the Louvre. In a conversation with J. Guenne, Matisse, who joined his class some months after Rouault, recalled that Moreau would tell them: "Don't just go to the museum; go down into the street as well."

At the School Rouault met the painters Léon Lehmann and Paul Baignères, who would subsequently become his faithful companions. Marquet and later Manguin and Puy also enrolled in Moreau's studio; ten years later, at the Salon d'Automne, together with Matisse they would be the inmates of the scandalously famous *cage aux fauves*. Rouault, who did not join the movement, was not present, although between 1903 and 1908 he participated actively in the foundation and organization of the Salon, the most important exhibition center of the time.

Rouault was one of Gustave Moreau's most restless pupils. His spirit dictated that a canvas was not to be painted as a game of construction which would be completed with a final touch. "I observed once," wrote Matisse to Isabelle Rouault, the artist's daughter, "that Rouault was at the far end of the studio with Maxence, near the washroom: while continuing to work, he waited until Maxence was thoroughly engrossed in what he was doing and then started jumping up and down and screeching like an insane monkey. Maxence said, 'You're disturbing me, Rouault'." Later, on recalling this episode, Rouault commented that his classmate was "very patient."

In 1894, encouraged by Moreau, Rouault entered for the Rome prize, but to no avail. The following year he obtained the Chenavard Prize under controversial circumstances, that is, after revision of the verdict of the jury, who had at first awarded the prize to a pupil of Bonnat's. Bonnat was one of Moreau's rival teachers and a highly influential academic painter. Rouault's canvas, *The Child Jesus among the Doctors*, was highly conventional in subject and format; nevertheless it was the first of his works to be acquired by the Musées de France. The influence of Moreau can clearly be seen here, specifically in Jesus' countenance, and also that of Rembrandt, which would be prominent during the artist's formative years. The painter and poet Évenepoel, one of Rouault's fellow pupils, describes in a letter to his father his enthusiasm for the canvas: "Yesterday, at the Chenavard exhibition, I experienced a feeling of admiration that no other modern painter has ever aroused in me. For the Chenavard Prize two pupils from our studio were designated to produce large format canvases of one of their sketches. These were Bussy and Rouault. Three pupils of Bonnat and Gérôme also entered. It was a genuine triumph. You can't possibly imagine the joy we felt and how contented I was, the more so because Rouault's work is a true masterpiece. . . . Our classmate, who is only 23 or 24 years old, has produced a truly admirable work. Bussy's canvas was ten times better than anything produced by our rival pupils, but everything was eclipsed by Rouault's. When I reached the hall it was deserted: only before this painting there was a compact group formed from all the pupils from the other studios. It was a total victory, and marks the beginning of the career of a true master. Everything I'm saying sounds a little pompous but, believe me, I was so moved that tears filled my eyes. Remember the name, for I can assure you that we haven't heard the last of it.''

On the strength of this triumph, Rouault entered again for the Rome Prize with *The Holy Women Mourn for Jesus*. Once again to no avail. By now fully aware of the personality of his pupil, Moreau advised him to quit the school: "Tell me, what are you doing in this Hell? Work at home on your own account.'' Rouault took Moreau's advice, but continued to show his former teacher his works, among them probably the great *Nighttime Landscape* (1897), now in the Musée d'Orsay.

In 1898 Moreau died of throat cancer. "He died with his brushes in his hand,'' wrote Rouault, ". . . he would accept nothing that might relieve his sufferings and dull his spirit.'' For Rouault Moreau's death was a terrible shock, and marked the beginning of a crisis that would last for several years. "It was then that I suffered one of my most violent crises and I began painting canvases of an offensive lyricism.'' Little is known about events of this time. His family left Paris for Algeria while he, in the company of his friend Bourbon, went in 1901 in search of Huysmans, who was in the Abbey of Liguge, with the idea of forming a community of Catholic artists. However, due to the climate of the time, markedly anticlerical and even anti-religious, the project was a precarious one; indeed, the law against associations approved by the French parliament at the beginning of the summer forced them to part company.

Back in Paris, Rouault worked with the same enthusiasm as when he was in the school studio. However, his state of health deteriorated suddenly in 1902, and he was forced to rest in Évian for several weeks. There, with the country light, everything changed: "Rest, the sky, and the snow cleansed my eyes . . . I felt somehow liberated and began to paint frantically.'' He ceased to paint in the manner that would ensure the approval of Gustave Moreau's collectors, and his art took a new direction, apparently to Rouault's surprise before anyone else's.

Ten years later Rouault wrote to the author André Suarès: "*Le père* Moreau used to reproach me for not sleeping enough, for being in constant vigil, night and day (and without being boastful, he didn't reproach many for the same defect). Yet, after his death I have continued to sleep little, and I don't reproach myself for this, since in this way I've learnt to appreciate better what my limits are . . . I've not been tempted to go too far, this doesn't concern me, but I know, to the extent that we can really know something, the terrain in which I have to live. Everything has its price . . . and if for the last ten years I've shunned all distractions, . . . I have this other joy: alone here . . .

I know that I breathe clear air and that my phobias will soon be transformed into creative joy...."

In 1903 the Musée Gustave Moreau was inaugurated. Rouault became curator of the museum with the help of Henri Rupp, Moreau's legatee and administrator of his house, donated to the state of France and from now onwards the artist's personal museum. In Moreau's library Rouault discovered a book which moved him deeply. Its author was the Catholic writer Léon Bloy. On March 16, 1904 Bloy wrote in his *Journal*: "I have been informed that the painter Georges Rouault, pupil of Gustave Moreau, has developed a passionate interest in my work. In his master's house he found *La femme pauvre*, which I had sent with this dedication: 'To Gustave Moreau, as revenge against M. Folantin.' This book has pierced Rouault's heart, causing a wound that will never heal. I tremble to think of the punishment that will befall the poor unfortunate."

Folantin is obviously a nickname that Bloy had coined for Huysmans, who had been a friend of his for many years. Rouault went to visit Bloy on the recommendation of their mutual friend Auguste Marguillier, and soon the painter showed the writer his canvas *The Child Jesus among the Doctors*. Bloy, in turn, expressed his enthusiastic approval.

One year later, however, Bloy's opinion changed ostensibly when he contemplated Rouault's latest works: "Second visit to the Salon d'Automne.... I discover Rouault's works which I had not previously seen. A great pity. He searches for a new way; unfortunately this artist, whom I considered capable of painting angels, seems now able only to conceive atrocious and vengeful caricatures. He has suffered such violent horror repercussions through the fault of bourgeois infamy that his art seems now to be fatally wounded." This reproach is somewhat surprising, however, in view of the fact that one characteristic of Bloy's books and articles is precisely that they abound in "vengeful caricatures" which cannot really be taken into consideration when it comes to evaluating the quality of the writer's work. Rouault had exhibited a watercolor in which he sought to pay homage to Bloy's portrait of the odious Poulot couple in *La femme pauvre*, but the reaction on the part of the author was undoubtedly quite the opposite to the one he had expected. Exasperated by his contemporaries, a fervent Catholic and little given to concessions, what Bloy expected from painting was pacification of the battles he fought in his writings. In matters of art his tastes were conventional; for many years he had admired the academic painter Henri de Groux, although eventually they fell out. "Ungrateful beggar" or "pilgrim of the absolute," as he called himself, Rouault's "new way" was something Bloy could never appreciate.

Indeed, Rouaut's watercolors depict beings of a repulsive nature. They are prostitutes, such as the *Girl with Mirror* (1906, Musée National d'Art Moderne de Paris) or personages convinced of their own importance, as can be seen in *Judges* and *Courtroom Scenes*, which were painted during the same period. In the prostitute pieces, the body is crowned by a face often reduced to a protruding, almost animal-like jaw which merges into the confusion of brushstrokes while the outline of their flesh is delimited by sturdy dark lines.

The lines and the colors are lively and masterful. The sinister faces of the judges are arranged according to an inverse balance: the lines are concentrated to emphasise their facial features, while their red togas are left in a diffuse light. These works are the affirmation of what Rouault would write later in his *Soliloques*: "Drawing is a flash of the alert spirit."

Rouault was a solicitous friend, and despite their differences of opinion his friendship with Bloy remained intact. On reading the latter's violent written diatribes, on following in his *Journal* the tumultuous evolution of their relationship, one finds it hard to believe that nothing fundamental placed them in conflict.

Bloy regularly sent the painter all his books; Rouault replied with promptness, as if moved by the impulse of a revelation. In 1912, having received his *Introduction à la vie de Mélanie*, he wrote: "Your book has vanquished my desire to speak to you of it; the deep emotion I feel has prevented me from employing normal terms on receiving such a treasure. I have not even read the book in its entirety, I am still on the first pages and here I wander as if through a delicious labyrinth where I have been lucky enough to escape from this foul-smelling life. And I do not wish to find my way out, I am afraid to see the litanies of sorrow and desperation heightened by divine support."

In 1905 Rouault made a decisive encounter in Léon Bloy's house. A young couple, Raïssa and Jacques Maritain, introduced themselves to the writer having read some of his books with enthusiasm. In *Les grands amitiés*, her book of memoirs, Raïssa gives a brief description of the atmosphere of the evenings they spent in Bloy's house: "How many times, in the following years, we saw Rouault at Bloy's house, standing against the wall, a slight smile on his closed lips, his gaze in the distance, his face apparently impassive but of a pallor that would increase until we began to speak of modern painting. Rouault would pale but keep a heroic silence until the end. And yet, despite the irreducible distance between them in matters of his art, Rouault remained faithful to Léon Bloy. It has been said that he sought in Bloy the very accusations against what he most loved that tormented his soul, not to reply to them in any way, but rather to try out against them the force of instinct which drove him towards the unknown and which would have to overcome all obstacles."

In 1912 Rouault and his family moved to Versailles, where they met up once again with the Maritains, with whom they had established a close friendship. Once a week Rouault had supper at their house; conversation often became a monologue in which the painter would talk about his activities, about Gustave Moreau, about the old masters and about contemporary painting. Marthe Rouault, whom he had married in 1908, was an excellent pianist; until the twenties she gave piano lessons in order to cover the economic needs of the family and safeguard her husband's independence. "Like Léon Bloy," wrote Raïssa Maritain, "Georges Rouault had an admirable woman at his side, patient in the face of adversity, and beautiful children ... who were both his joy and his torment. For their sake and for that of his own well-being, could he renounce the purity of the artist's conscience and produce painting that would find a ready market? What tragic depth those debates had! We were fortunate to become a little familiar with it." When Bloy died in 1917, Jacques Maritain became the person with whom Rouault could communicate most freely. Art and religion were the preoccupations they had in common. Ten years younger than Rouault, Maritain said of his friend that he was "the artist in the pure state." Rouault had embraced the Christian religion when he was about twenty-five years old, after a long personal search, assisted by Father Vallée, whom he had met at the house of his friend René Piot when he was a pupil at the studio of Gustave Moreau. The latter, too, had a religious concept of art that contributed to push him in this direction. Furthermore, his frequent contacts with Bloy, of a fine sensitivity in religious matters, also fortified his vision.

Maritain was a former pupil of Bergson's; a philosopher by training and a writer, his was a fine, precise spirit, but his main quality was the attention he was able to pay his fellows. He was the first writer and friend who truly accepted Rouault's work during the most difficult years of the artist's life.

Several years after the death of her husband, Marthe Rouault was persuaded to write a few pages for a homage to Maritain: "...A great example hovered over us, made even more acute by the memory of his total comprehension of the work of Georges Rouault at a time when few people were aware of its true value....We often went to visit them with our small troupe (the Rouaults had four children) on Sunday afternoons. At times he must have considered us a nuisance, although he never said anything. An infinite number of intellectuals would gather there, eager to talk of philosophy. My husband felt happy in this select company and, as they grew up, the children became more and more interested....."

Maritain entertained clerics and theologians, writers, poets and artists; besides Rouault, Chagall was the painter he knew best. On the basis of his conversations with Rouault, in 1920 Maritain published a major work with the generic title of *Art and Scholastics*, which features one of the first studies of the painter. In his opinion, "as the saint consumes in himself the work of passion, so the poet consumes in himself the work of creation." Although too modest a man to appropriate this idea for himself, Rouault must have understood it clearly, since it refers to his religious feeling. He lived concentrated on his paintings. All the seriousness he exuded at times came from his studio.

"Aware of his greatness as an artist," writes Raïssa Maritain, "and respectful of his secrets, we never dared ask him to show us what he was doing. This itself made him more willing to communicate openly. Later we witnessed how indiscretion horrified him: one day we came back together from Bourg-la-Reine, where Léon Bloy was living since he had left Montmartre and Rue de la Barre. Ricardo Viñes was with us. Either out of sincere interest, or possibly because this was considered the done thing as far as painters were concerned, Viñes asked Rouault if he could see his studio. Rouault growled in reply, became morose and from that day onwards deeply detested the poor musician whom, of course, he never admitted into his studio." When this account was published, Rouault was at pains to make it clear that he had excellent relations with the famous composer, whom he truly esteemed, but he had not wanted to show him his studio since it was then in a state of thorough chaos because of the work in which he was currently engaged.

There can be no doubt that Rouault took what he did very seriously, but because of his tactlessness he could not take himself seriously; he attached far more importance to his painting than to himself. Those who knew him intimately recall above all his candor and his ingenuousness, as if his character changed as from the moment when he no longer had to face up to the demands of his art. In 1921, when Éditions Gallimard requested a self-portrait for the cover of a short book they were about to publish about his work, Rouault obliged by sending them a painting of himself wearing a clown's hat. When he saw the book published with the hat carefully removed, he hardly flinched; indeed, he even viewed it with a certain elation. By that time he had already begun to use the ambivalent figure of the clown, in which he probably found the best image for his activities among his contemporaries. However, a subtle mixture of self-irony, cynicism and a bitter philosophy of existence is not merely a literary symbol; it is also, and above all, a medium through which better to capture reality. In a letter dated 1905 to the art critic Édouard Schuré, Rouault explained with special clarity the reasons which had prompted him to choose a repertoire of subjects which, apart from Picasso in his Blue Period, only he had exploited:

"... For me, from the end of a beautiful day in which the first evening star that shines in the firmament makes my heart sink, I don't know why, I have deliberately let flow a whole poetics from here. That caravan of nomads parked along the road, the old consumptive horse that grazes on the thin grass, the old clown sitting on the running-board of his trailer darning his shining, multicolored costume, that *contrast* between brilliant, dazzling things, made to amuse, and that life of an *infinite sadness* when seen slightly from above... Later I have extended all this. I have seen clearly that the 'clown' was I, was us, almost all of us... That *sumptuous sequin covered costume* is given to us by life, we are all *clowns to a greater or lesser extent*, we all wear a 'sequin covered costume,' but if someone surprises us as I have surprised the old clown, oh! Who would then dare say that he has not been overwhelmed, down to the pit of his stomach, by an immense pity. My defect (defect perhaps ... in any case, for me it is an abyss of suffering ...) is that I *strip everyone of their sequin covered costume*, be they kings or emperors. I want to see the soul of the man standing before me ... and the greater he is and the more he is glorified by humanity, the more I fear for his soul.... To extract all one's art from the gaze of a wicked old woman or of a mountebank (man or horse) is a matter either of 'insane pride' or of 'perfect humility,' if one is made to do so.... In August I shall probably at last be able to travel a bit, and I have the strongest feeling that I shall extract all my art from life and from the emotions with which it provides me."

Aware of the risk that his painting would be misunderstood, Rouault made a number of practical comments: "If the judges in my canvases are such lamentable figures, it is because they represent the anguish I feel for a human being who is about to judge other men. If I confuse the head of the judge with the head of the accused, this error simply reflects my perplexity. Judges as such I cannot condemn." At the same time, the artist was painting his first versions of the *Holy Countenance*, followed by other motifs, equally religious, which would later appear much more frequently in his work.

By painting Rouault understood harmony. He applied this term to color, form and drawing. He saw painting as a whole, not only from canvas to canvas but also in the way his oeuvre evolved throughout his life. For him a work is an organism whose parts cannot be dissociated. Anecdote has little room here. His paintings are never observations of reality directly reapplied, since Rouault never set out to fix detail. He could not retain in his painting what he saw the moment he saw it. The dexterity that Delacroix recommended has no raison d'être in Rouault's work: "To tauten the will is not enough," he wrote to Suarès, "one must also have the pictorial *means* by which to achieve the anticipated results."

Rouault's first major exhibition was held in the Galerie Druet in 1910. Here he showed his paintings — his girls, his mountebanks and his first judges as well as several ceramics. Between 1903 and 1908 he painted very rarely in oil. The technique he preferred was watercolor heightened by pastel and gouache. He did not adopt oil painting until 1909, after first trying out tempera, which for him lacked consistency. By this time he was already admired and helped by a few major collectors, such as Marcel Sembat (whose exquisite collection was donated to the Musée de Grenoble) and, shortly afterwards, Doctor Girardin, who left part of his collection to the city of Paris.

It is observed that in Rouault's work the matter of the painting is very particular. In 1907 his fauve friends changed direction; some of them switched to the cubist experience. Rouault, on the other hand, was too engrossed in his own research, which continued to disconcert critics. Even Apollinaire did not quite know where to place him at first, and included him in an article on Cubism for lack of anywhere else to situate him. Rouault appeared as one of the best artists. The writers Jacques Rivière and Alain-Fournier, guided by the painter and critic André Lhote, attempted to help him. Having visited the Salon d'Automne in 1908, Jacques Rivière wrote to André Lhote:

"The only one to have produced something really good is Rouault. This time he has . . . so long as he continues. There are three paintings of nude women, some more finished than others. The first is reminiscent of those of Les Indépendants. The second is very good, with its large, fine forms, chaotic and yet linked, and with its somber, wine-like tones that shine dully. Finally, the third one exudes a sweetness, a union and a depth which are most admirable. The outline, ever simple, is suggested by the masses and is deliciously pure. The color itself is applied carefully, slowly, definitively. My liking for this is almost unrestricted, and in the Salon there is nothing that even begins to approach such power and originality."

The following year Jacques Rivière, who in the meantime had once more made contact with the artist, wrote in the same vein, although he expressed less specialized considerations. "On Monday I saw Rouault, who brought his canvases. We were together for an hour and a quarter, an hour and a quarter during which he explained to me his exalted concepts of Christianity.

I can't repeat everything he said since I don't have time. Only this: 'Who knows if I'm not preparing myself to paint a *Combat between the Virtues and the Vices*? In which case, should I not have to study vice?'"

One day Rouault would say that "it took the critics thirty years to discover the bite of sin in my work." The "monsters" who emerged from his brush — circus artists, cabaret dancers, clowns, acrobats and, at a remove from the world of the circus and mountebanks, his prostitutes, his courtroom scenes and his vagrants who wander through the suburbs — would one day cause him to be considered a descendant of Goya and Daumier.

In a study from 1929, André Malraux lucidly observed that "despite what is erroneously called 'picturesque' in Rouault's subject matter, for him the model does not exist: it is a possibility, it is what he will transform into writing, that writing of Rouault's, at times dense and hard, at times fragmented like the stained-glass windows of Chartres. Here each being is reduced to what he can be after a tragic meditation on himself. . . . Nothing could show better that the work of Rouault is little subject to the outside world or to comparison to canvases by other painters. In the Palais there are judges by Daumier, in Spain, mountebanks by Goya, in the city outskirts landscapes by Vlaminck; there are none of Rouault's judges, girls or clowns outside his canvases, just as Grünewald's characters have never existed outside his books. These are not human beings; they are signs of a plastic order."

Contrary to the theories that have been devised subsequently regarding the artistic movements of this period, the disappearance of the motif in painting was not an imperative that concerned all modern artists. Rouault did not only closely follow the artistic revolution of 1905 and 1906 (Apollinaire recalls in his chronicles of the Salons that the painter was highly indignant at the unfair rejection of a canvas sent by Matisse), but also took active part in this revolution of the gaze by introducing in his works a dramatic amplification found neither in the Fauves nor the Cubists. When in March 1925 an exhibition of Rouault's work was held in Berlin, a German critic wrote the following in the *Berliner Tageblatt*: "A revolutionary discovery amidst the aesthetic disorder that has reigned among us for ten years. We were told that it was the ecstasy of the German soul that drove so many artists to scoff at form in order better to be able to express what they felt. We were assured that those who wanted to understand nothing of this revolution were decrepit, fossilized old men. And now we have this exhibition by Rouault, in which we can see from where all the ecstatic German artists have taken the means to express themselves. Everything comes from Rouault! The biting feature, the decomposed faces, the composition which always features two or three characters. Even the technique, with the dark brushstrokes in black and the smudges of watercolor thrown here and there to clarify everything."

It is not true that German Expressionism comes from Rouault; even so, this observation is no less revealing of the effect his works must have produced on the general public at that time.

Rouault was highly secretive about his way of painting. His technique must therefore have been a matter of intrigue. Nobody was allowed to enter his studio; even his family was invited in only on exceptional occasions. Nevertheless, it seems certain that he did not work in an "ecstatic" way. To realize this one need only contemplate the numerous faces he painted — the *Heads of Clowns* from 1910-1920, the *Saints* from the following years, the major versions of the *Holy Countenance* and the *Women Types* he executed until the end of his life. In the midst of this abundance of faces, there cannot be many more than ten portraits over a total of two thousand finished and catalogued paintings that Rouault executed in the presence of live models. The engraved portraits for his *Souvenirs intimes*, those of Verlaine, Baudelaire, Gustave Moreau, Huysmans, Léon Bloy and Suàres, were realized from photographs and documents as well as from the impressions he retained of these and of the people he had known or with whom he continued to have dealings. They are probably the best portraits in existence of the subjects in question; furthermore, it is possible today to verify their likeness, since we now know for certain which documents Rouault used, for example, a photograph by Carjat of Baudelaire's and Verlaine's death masks. Above all, however, they are highly faithful to the spirit of the subjects' work and manage to capture the aura of each personality. Yet, while Rouault's choice must have been dictated by a strong sense of personal identification, these portraits are no more elaborated than those of the vast series *Types and Faces*, all of which were painted without a model.

It is surprising to learn that despite Rouault's close identification with both the work and temperament of Cézanne, he painted mostly from memory and hardly ever from nature. With the exception of his landscapes prior to 1903, all his paintings are from the imagination, and their true motif is the correspondence between colors, forms and expression of the figures. *Toque noire, robe rouge, font belles taches de couleur* is the title of one of his major texts on painting. Rouault had understood that "the tiniest brushstroke or *frottis* teach us more than so many indigestible tomes; on the other hand, this does not mean that there is no hierarchy or inner order." An "inner order" that fully coincides with the "inner necessity" that allowed Kandinsky to conceive and define abstract art.

Some of Rouault's contemporaries have emphasized the painter's religious commitment over and above his gifts as a colorist and his sense of harmony and outline. If he had never committed his art to his faith, his oeuvre would not exist, a fact which was only reluctantly accepted and led at times to his being looked upon with suspicion. Nevertheless, more than a theory, a religion is a gaze directed at the world, a tense, organised attention to things. Rouault was interested above all in man, in his body and his face, which he attempted to see better. The fury of his early works is due possibly to impatience with life, a lack of satisfaction which he overcame not through satisfaction with his work — for Rouault was very rarely satisfied —, but through the search for this satisfaction. Being the Christian he was, he did not deceive himself with false hopes, he knew that he could only prepare himself for this happiness. One of his major works, which occupies the center of his creation as a whole by virtue both of its chronological position and its importance in terms of his artistic development, is the self-portrait of 1925, now in the Musée National d'Art Moderne de Paris, which he had modestly titled *L'apprenti ouvrier* (The Apprentice Artisan). This portrait is remarkable for its perturbing veracity. The background blue and green tones, opposed to the light which sharply outlines the face, evoke a violent concentration. The canvas is a combination between precision and vagueness, as if an even stronger image were about to emerge from it. It is like a mirror which, through the action of painting, had retained the memory of the personage visible there: not of his image but of his reality. It expresses an effort at self knowledge, frequently found in painters, although there are few examples that achieve such intensity of attention. In his *Inquisiciones*, Jorge Luis Borges includes a study of a preoccupation he encountered in several passages of Léon Bloy's *Journal*. It concerns a proposition by St. Paul (Corinthians I, XIII, 12): "Now we see in the mirror, in the darkness; but then we shall see each other face to face. Now I know in part, but then I shall know that I am known." It is unlikely that Rouault would not have seen here an image of that corner of Paradise he sought, or that he did not perceive that every face is a mirror.

Over the years Rouault's technique developed visibly. After his rupture with "realist" painting, his work consisted mostly of watercolors. This style, in which subtlety of color would be the same as that of matter, would evolve towards the use of thicker material, although there is a general consensus that the evolution of his work as a whole was a natural phenomenon, closer to the regular growth of trees — as if driven by the energy that makes them grow — than to the unforeseeable logic behind the development of a work of art. It is highly likely that such regularity was due to his feeling for matter and his tenacity. In 1910 Jacques Rivière wrote to André Lhote:

"Rouault hasn't stopped talking from 5 o'clock until seven thirty. He's a most congenial man. Amongst the notes he brought with him there's a phrase I find particularly moving: "*collaborer avec la matière.*" He attempts to find links with the artisan tradition of the Middle Ages, or rather to recover it, aided in his endeavor by a ferocious individualism."

During the twenties, and parallel to the realization of his large engravings in black and white, color, which cannot be disassociated from matter, came to occupy a privileged position in his painting. Moreau had already emphasized his attention to matter; furthermore, his gifts as a colorist had been well known for some time. Regarding the main figure in his *The child Jesus among the Doctors*, Évenepoel concluded the aforementioned letter to his father with the following words: " . . . he is absolutely pure, innocent, blond, bathed in a sweet amber light; they (the doctors) are totally somber, violent, reddish-black, and their gazes are sharply penetrating; the multitude, to left and right, boisterous and lively . . . has on its flanks heads of a profound nature: there are powerful reds and greens, arcades that merge high up with the twilight, a background of primitive city; a Virgin Mary, who approaches radiantly from the right on a nimbus; and the whole composition, when one steps back from it, is a gem in itself, a mosaic of emerald, ruby, topaz and amethyst. . . . " Rouault kept this gift for color thanks to his work, and he put it to use not only in his paintings but also in the considerable number of art ceramic pieces he produced between 1906 and 1912 in Méthey's studio, and in the prints (monotypes) from the press he installed in his own studio. Black ink and fire allowed him to satisfy not only his need for an immediately physical artisan contact with the materials he used for his art, but also, on coming into close contact with matter, to remind himself that he maintained a congenital relationship with fire and color.

One night in April 1913 Rouault wrote to Suarès: "I think I've found a matter, a matter... why should I try to qualify it? A true matter; for example, I defy you to tell me what it's made of... I have the impression that if that head of a clown or of Pierrot were to adopt a grave demeanor... (which it already has through the sense of the drawing and of the matter), it would be something exceptional (the Christ of the Passion, for example; that's what my matter is made for). I must say that these pieces have been fired eight or ten times. There's a dish which is misshapen but, too bad, it will still be fired twice more. I won't show you anything, neither you nor anyone else... I'm searching for a matter, and it would also be impossible to say how it's made and how to remake it.... I think,... in the midst of massacres, of fires and of horrors, I've retained from the basement where I was born, in my eyes and in my spirit, the fleeting matter that good fire fixes and inlays." This subterranean, almost volcanic, activity was the result of a lively curiosity and of an uncommon visual memory and sense of observation.

The same year, on returning home from a stroll in the Parc de Versailles, Rouault once again wrote to André Suarès, who had become his privileged confidant: "During my stroll I've seen marvelous snow effects against an extraordinarily varied and inconceivably delicate sky starting with sulphur, verdigris, then a series of tender pinks like flower petals, and finally the whole range of grays and pinks."

Contrary to what one might have expected, however, his observations did not result in a landscape painting. The *Old King* (1937), in the Carnegie Institute, Pittsburgh, is the fictitious portrait of a personage whom Rouault almost certainly never knew. The sheen of his face, the red of his garments and the green and blue tones of the background create the impression of a sunset with human body. The difference between what belongs to the spectacle of nature and to the expressive powers of man is rather vague here. Pierre Courthion, in his major biography of Rouault published in 1962, says the following: "Matisse liked this painting very much. He had hung a reproduction of it in Cimiez, in the corridor of his house, beside that of *The Man with his Ear Cut Off*. And when together we contemplated these two sheets of color, he commented to me that when compared to the dense, powerful painting of Rouault, Van Gogh's self-portrait had the air of an XVIII-century canvas."

The same year that he painted *Old King*, Rouault was offered a hall in the "Les Maîtres de l'Art Indépendent" exhibition at the Petit Palais, a subsidiary of the International Exhibition. The public discovered forty-two paintings and what Rouault had done since the end of the war. It was a retrospective exhibition, gathering together older, more somber works, and those produced between 1918 and 1937. Although Rouault was forced against his better judgement to accept the juxtaposition of two periods which for him were completely different, the response was excellent. The critic Waldemar George published a major article in which he expressed his amazement that such important work could have hitherto been ignored. Rouault's reputation, which had gradually broken out from the circle of his friends and admirers, was by now considerable. The Italian critic and art historian Lionello Venturi also discovered Rouault and, on the basis of numerous interviews with the artist at his home, wrote several books about him, the first of which appeared five years later in the United States. In 1939 a retrospective of his engravings was held in the Museum of Modern Art of New York, followed by a major retrospective of his paintings in 1945. In France, the writer Marcel Arland, who came into regular contact with the painter as from 1930, published several articles which would assist young artists to understand Rouault's work.

When war was declared, Rouault fled from Paris to Beaumont-sur-Sarthe together with his daughters Geneviève and Agnès. However, the exodus forced them one year later to seek refuge in Golfe-Juan. He worked in the kitchen, the brightest room in the house. When they returned to Beaumont they found that the Germans had ransacked their home, damaged drawings and documents and destroyed letters and dedicated books. In contrast to what he did in the previous war, however, this time he produced only one work related to the world conflict: a scaffold to which he gave the title *Man is a Wolf to Man*, in Latin.

During these difficult years Rouault finished numerous important works. In 1942 he signed *Pierrot the Aristocrat*, which by virtue of its luster and discreetly monumental quality is the synthesis of his works. These works leave no doubt as to the difficulty Rouault encountered in taking his paintings where he wanted: "What I regret is not having a second life in order to take certain works to a certain point." Nevertheless, these scruples were to act in his favor in the lawsuit which immediately after the war ended was to place him in conflict with the person who had been his main dealer, Ambroise Vollard.

In 1917 Ambroise Vollard, who had known Rouault for over ten years, told the artist of his desire to buy his studio. Vollard was at the time one of the most prestigious art dealers in Paris. In a sketch of him published in 1940 in the *Nouvelle Revue Française*, Suàres wrote: "He has been the man of Manet, Redon, Gauguin, and many others, of Bonnard, Rouault, Vuillard and Picasso." In 1901 he began to exhibit the latter's works, and as from 1890 it was possible to find in his gallery paintings by Degas, Renoir and Cézanne. In the windows of his gallery, then in Rue Lafitte, Rouault had seen Gauguin's *Christ jaune*, a work which deeply impressed him and which probably served as a source of inspiration for his own *Crucifixions*.

The artist and the dealer first met in Méthey's studio around 1906, when Rouault was producing art ceramic pieces. They must have been on excellent terms, for in 1917 in Saumur, where the dealer was living, Vollard entrusted the painter with the protection of the paintings in his private collection. In 1917 the "pact" was made by which Rouault became linked to Vollard for thirty years. The dealer presented him with an "all or nothing" alternative:

either he would cede to him all the canvases in his studio (over seven hundred) or none. The artist accepted on the condition that he be allowed to finish the works he had started, even though the task might take him the rest of his life. No more was ever said about this agreement. During the twenties Vollard installed Rouault's studio on the large ground floor of his residence in Rue Martignac, where the artist was to work day and night. In a text from 1924, Jacques Maritain revealed his understanding of the true advantages Rouault gained from this far from banal relationship with his dealer: "Everything that affects him and everything he does are plunged into secrets, he is driven by a ferocious desire to hide, for this reason he exhibits so rarely, and he has M. Ambroise Vollard's mercantile instincts to thank for the fact that a dense fog keeps his work concealed from the gaze of the uninitiated. In fact, he belongs to the category of the timidly explosive. A Parisian on his mother's side, but a Breton Celt on his father's, in his inner self, in the inaccessible regions of his heart, he stores intangible treasures of dream and nostalgia, of suffering and blue, which contact with his fellow man wounds and oppresses."

Indeed, the relations between the painter and his dealer were not exempt from occasional frictions. Vollard overburdened Rouault. He requested paintings, but above all he commissioned books from him. The first of these works is *Les réincarnations du Père Ubu* (with the text by Vollard), published in 1932. This was followed by *Le cirque de l'étoile filante*, published in 1938, *Passion*, by André Suàres, and finally *Miserere* (printed in 1927 but not published until 1948, with a preface by Rouault).

"His great editions have occupied all his work and leisure time," wrote Suàres. "... All those who have seen *Passion* must agree that whether one likes or dislikes Rouault's art, or mine, this book is unique. Those who should follow him are no fewer. Vollard would repeat unceasingly, with all the right in the world: 'Books such as these have never been produced, and never will be again.' He was right. ... There could never have been a truer, more constant desire for perfection than his; he deceived himself, his enemies would say. That remains to be seen. His passion for the book, as he conceived it, was infinitely greater than his love for paintings. He wanted the book to be the masterpiece of a great painter."

Suàres wrote these lines in homage to Vollard, who died tragically in a road accident in July 1939. Early in September the dealer's heirs sealed the doors to Rouault's studio. The artist was thus brutally barred from his works and deprived of any possibility, essential to him, of returning to earlier works. Furthermore, the circumstances of the declaration of war turned this drama into an inferno. Years later, recalling these times, he wrote to his friend Georges Chabot: "In 1939, an ill-fated year for peoples and individuals, I saw snatched from me my large pigeonholes and hundreds of 'pictorial notes,' some light but more often grave, with which I had been in permanent contact whenever it suited me, Sundays and holidays, even in August, when the temperature reached 43°C. I would sooner be deprived of air, of light, of wine, of coffee, of white bread or of my uncommon and precious friendships than of *mon clavier pictural*."

A lawsuit was begun that lasted four years. Rouault finally emerged victorious in 1947. He recovered all his works, with the exception of a hundred or so which Vollard's heirs had imprudently transferred, and then made the decision to dispose of those he could not suitably finish, burning three hundred and fifteen of them before the court tipstaff. This totally unexpected gesture acquired him immediate and spectacular fame. The astonished press heaped praise upon him. What had been Rouault's drama, the demise of his dealer and the confiscation of a work begun over forty years earlier, was resolved by a court decision. (The artist had gathered together watercolors and paintings from before 1914 and had retouched them; furthermore, he had kept his prints in the hope of one day publishing them.) The verdict conceded him the moral right to his work and allowed him to have it at his disposal in order to complete it.

Quite some time after the liberation of France, *Miserere* was finally published and exhibited in a Parisian gallery. Begun immediately after the death of his father in 1912, which occurred a few days after Rouault and his family had moved to Versailles, and continued during World War I, *Miserere* is a reflection on man and on the disasters of war. Rouault now spent even more time than ever beside the presses, constantly correcting what they bring him and unceasingly modifying the copper plates (on occasions up to fifteen times) in order to find the exact tones and light and to obtain, after over a decade of effort, a result that would in no way betray the amount of time invested in its creation.

Miserere is considered to be the artist's masterpiece, the work to which he devoted most time and effort and which undoubtedly synthesizes his creation as a whole. The nuances of black and gray, which the camera is incapable of capturing, are so subtle and harmonious that they are the profound manifestation of his mastery over matter and color. It is the visual equivalent of horror, an inner witness to the effects of war in which Baudelaire's crepuscular atmosphere and the *tristesse majestueuse* that Racine sought in his preface to *Bérénice* come together. The scenes succeed each other in silence as in a very slow-motion film in which each frame is the result of years of work. Yet while the motifs are often somber, they are never sinister. The work is a reverie made up of precise memories and visions that refer to the most important stages in man's destiny. Kings, criminals, mothers, "ladies of noble birth," families of beggars, prostitutes, clowns and corpses gather round the Virgin and Child in the baptism of Jesus, his crucifixion and his resurrection. The book's fifty-eight plates endow the events with an intensity at once intimate and anonymous. Of all his works, these are the ones best known all the world over. There can be no doubt that awareness of the horrors of World War II has facilitated understanding of *Miserere*. The gallery in which the work was first exhibited in 1948 was crammed with visitors the whole time it was on display. His work imposes itself like that of a "visionary." The visionary that André Suarès, who died that same year, saw in his friend almost forty years before.

In 1948 Rouault moved into a large flat opposite the belfry of the Gare de Lyon, where he gladly received artists, art critics and, not without protest, a few photographers when, as we have seen, in the past he accepted the visit of only a handful of close friends, since he did not want to be disturbed. In the lightest room, whose windows he had made opaque with emery paper except for a small rectangle through which he could see what time it was, he painted and meditated without pressure being placed upon him, and thought about his painting and his grandchildren. The fortunate outcome of the lawsuit freed him from a number of worries. His work now developed following a range of increasingly warm colors.

His painting entered its final period, the luminous and tranquil period of *Christian Nocturne* and *End of Autumn III*, both from 1952. The calm and the strange imminence of happiness create that sensation of intensity felt after a summer storm in nature. Jacques Maritain, who followed the evolution of Rouault's work throughout his life, wrote in a preface published in New York in 1952: "To what can it be due that when we contemplate certain works of art we are aware of having received 'an immortal wound?' Rouault's painting is exclusively painting, preoccupied only with the passionate search for ways of satisfying the demands of pictorial matter, for sensitivity of the eye, for the wisest and most refined precision in technical media. And, at the same time, he extracts his life force from the intimate universe of the soul, from the depths of the inner vision and poetic intuition, obscurely capturing, in emotion, both the subjectivity of the painter and the mystery of the visible world."

The matter covering his canvases has by now become very thick. An inattentive eye might find here that precision is sacrificed to an immoderate use of oil color. Indeed, his paintings consist of a greater number of coats and, as a consequence, many more nuances of color and light. *Sara* (1956), one of his last, is the face of a woman whose matter has been worked in such a way that it appears to be a colored bas-relief. The flesh-color of the cheeks dominates the decorative motif which acts as a frame, as if the face were emerging through the surface of the painting. By force of the demands of the search of the inner image Rouault pursues, the matter of his painting becomes transformed. This presence of the pictorial matter is the manifestation of his creative thought. Rouault works with his hands and his eyes, which control and evoke, rather than with reasoned formulae. Rouault cannot conceive in his spirit, but before his eyes, materially and without doctrine, with a single memory. In the presence of such canvases one is forced to assume that he spent many years on them before signing them. They are the ripe fruit of active sedimentation of the color which has quickly run over the limits of the initial drawing. In the catalog for the Rouault retrospective in Cologne (1983), Siegfried Gohr describes him as "a painter who thinks with color."

Parallel to his activities as a painter, Rouault always wrote as a distraction, either when he had finished work or when he could not paint. Part of his poetic output was put together in a series of luxury editions; his accounts, memoirs and complex personal reflections, elaborated to the extent that they acquired the density of prose poems, were the object of special editions, often illustrated, or were published in journals. The essence of his writings was collected in a small pocket edition published by Bernard Dorival, some years ago, under the title *Sur l'art et sur la vie*. Browsing through it, the reader is unaware of the innumerable corrections that preceded the definitive version. In his manuscripts and letters a joyful and generous handwriting covers the paper and floods the margins, often reaching the very edge of the leaf, possibly through fear of leaving too much blank space. The long hours spent silently in his studio propitiated the formation of his ideas, developed in phrases as his painting evolved on paper, reacting to the form of the words and their colors as vividly as in the background. His way of writing often has something of an incantation reminiscent of his *chansons de routes*, and comes near to nonsense through the clear predominance of rhythm, which acquires its own meaning.

If his writings had the density of his paintings, his letters often possess the vivacity and the exact notation of his drawings and sketches for *Miserere*. From the Moreau period until the final years, those who came into contact with him were deeply impressed by the burning conviction of his declarations.

On the cover of Pierre Courthion's monograph, a photograph depicts him seated, looking straight at an interlocutor who is before him but whom we cannot see, and attempting to give shape to his words with a lively movement of his hands. Rouault liked to be heard, but disliked being asked questions. After a visit to André Malraux, with a wry smile he bemoaned the fact that for the first time in his life he had been unable to utter a single word. With close friends Rouault was a lively, loquacious man, *"le plus joyeux drille que la terre ait jamais porté"* (the jolliest fellow the earth has ever given birth to), as he liked to describe himself in the face of those who reproached him for his "mauvais charactère," and added "...but painting, my dear Mediterraneans, is not simply that delicate or vulgar dish hanging on the wall. And joy is not simply a happy arabesque, a harmonious rhythm in a serene sky."

On reading his poems and comparing them with the legends which, between 1910 and 1918, he inscribed below the figures in his albums, in which he ridiculed the "bourgeois," we see that he knew how to modulate irony from ferocity to tenderness. Furthermore, his humor allowed him to make fun of himself. The reader is struck by the quality of his language: the simplest vocabulary even for the most difficult concepts combined with an abundance of images in a style which, when he uses poetry, takes the form of a small four-line composition, and becomes a simple, fluid and dense prose in which he speaks of his memories.

Rouault was dominated by an active and mobile curiosity, an ever alert spirit incapable of idleness, and was so eager to progress that sometimes he did not immediately recognize works of his he had not seen for some time. He was concerned not so much with finished work as with work still to be done.

During the retrospective which took place successively in Brussels, Amsterdam and Paris in 1952, Jean Cassou, founder of the Musée National d'Art Moderne, took him through the exhibition halls and recalls that he was surprised to see how Rouault expressed his astonishment at certain of his own works. After the evening the Centre Catholique des Intellectuels Français had organised for him at the Palais de Chaillot in June 1951, a Japanese journalist wrote that the artist had the feeling that the event was not for him. One might imagine him rather like Charlie Chaplin, searching in the assembly for the true beneficiary of the celebration, unable to conceive that it could be he himself.

In 1957 exhaustion forced him to stop painting. In his study he contemplated the paintings he had left there, saddened by the fact that he now lacked the strength to work on them. Nevertheless, he had the satisfaction of seeing how major retrospectives of his were being organized all over the world and how he was flooded with requests for works for further shows. In New York, Zurich, Venice, all over Europe and Japan, exhibitions succeeded one another.

Days after his death, an illustrated weekly published a photograph showing him engrossed in his work in his last studio. With both hands he lifts a painting above a table covered with other still unfinished works. The caption says that this was the first time the artist had been photographed at work. This is not exactly true, however: in another photograph, published in the magazine *Le Point* in 1944, Rouault contemplates a *Holy Countenance*, the pigment of which still appears to be wet. His horizontal way of painting, which allowed him to obtain a perspective from above, was characteristic more of an artisan than of an artist. The purpose of the easel was above all to present the painting, exhibit its supreme surface. A painting placed on a table is like an object which the artisan turns around in his hands until it has the required appearance, color, texture and weight.

All the *savoir-faire* that goes into artisan work is present in that of Rouault. When during his adolescence he worked as an apprentice in a master glazier's workshop, he undoubtedly proceeded in this way. The days he spent, year after year, before the kilns must have resembled the days he spent painting and engraving, and this behavior would suffice to show that Rouault was not a romantic artist. True to the hallowed phrase, his genius was the fruit of constant labor. However, gravity did not exclude either clarity or a certain joyfulness in his expression. The "joie persistante" with which he managed to imbue his paintings emanated from a spirit that preferred humble realities to great tragic impulses: "I do not believe," he wrote in *Le Point*, "either in theories or in the enormous, vague ideas to be found in the extraterrestrial world and which possess neither life nor viable form. I am particularly horrified by that wandering of thought and action which results in that clammy, sticky and facile idealism which makes corners soft and drawing inconsistent, which solves everything, explains everything. Such is my horror of this that I prefer cynicism, the most grotesque or most violent realism. For me, however much more imagination one has, however more one rides on dreams, the more need there is to be a realist; to develop gifts of stringent observation in order to store shapes and harmonies we see every day; to exercise in knowing them better; to play with them. One becomes enriched, then divested, if conceded this grace."

Similarly, Rouault said that for those who want to live, constant observation of nature is as essential as breathing: "I, my dear critic, am a WITNESS and, alas, an ACTOR, to a much greater extent than you could ever imagine, not a benevolent observer, and for this reason I may be allowed to add, at times I am trapped between dream and reality in areas far beyond the reaches where you move."

* * *

The years that have passed since Rouault's death allow us now to consider his work as an indissoluble whole. The recent publication of the catalog of his engravings and, immediately afterwards, of his paintings, has confirmed the richness of the artist's pictorial repertoire and contributed to greater understanding of the astonishing cohesion of his oeuvre. From his first watercolors to his last oil paintings, the effort he poured into his work would suffice to justify his rebellious temperament. The painter Desvallières said of him that "he did everything he possibly could not to arrive." Indeed, Rouault decided to paint more than to live; he preferred to apply his consciousness and his memories to form, to matter and to color in pursuit of the achievement he called harmony.

In 1963 his widow and his children donated around a thousand unfinished paintings, which the artist had left in his studio, to the state of France. The following year they were exhibited in the Salon Carré in the Louvre, the same hall where seventy years previously the works of the "masters" had been presented which Rouault, following the advice of Gustave Moreau, had studied and admired so much. His "unfinished" works, even more than the ones he signed, reveal all the freshness of his "alert spirit" and of his "modernity" (to use a term that would have amused him). On contemplating them, the observer appreciates all the vivacity of his spirit, his daring forms and colors. He undoubtedly mistrusted his gifts; he preferred a more completed form, able to rival the painting which had preceded him, efficient by virtue of its capacity to last rather than of its power to please. In 1971, the exhibition held in Paris on the occasion of the centenary of his birth confirmed the breadth and depth of the oeuvre which Rouault produced during an over sixty years of activity. Today it might be said that we still have a long way to go if we are to imagine all the richness of his work. The numerous exhibitions that have been held all over the world after his death, while giving the measure of this richness, remind us nevertheless that Rouault's work has yet to reveal all its meaning.

Biography

1871   May 27. The city of Paris, dominated by the Commune, is attacked by the artillery of the Versailles forces. During this attack, Georges-Henri Rouault is born in the basement of no. 51, Rue de la Villette; his mother was Marie-Louise Champdavoine and his father, a cabinet maker, Alexandre Rouault.

1881   Georges Rouault, who reveals precocious artistic gifts, is given his first lesson in art by his maternal grandfather, Alexandre Champdavoine, an admirer of Daumier, Courbet and Manet, who, at that time, were ridiculed by the bourgeois elite.

1885   He studies at the evening classes in the École des Arts Décoratifs.

1885-1890 He works in the glazier Tamoni's workshop and later in that of Hirsch. Albert Bernard proposes he make the stained-glass windows for the École de Pharmacie on the basis of his cartoons. Rouault turns this proposition down and decides to devote himself to painting.

1890   December 3. He enters the École National Supérieure des Beaux-Arts (the studio of Élie Delaunay).

1892   Delaunay dies, and his place is taken by Gustave Moreau. Rouault studies under him, as do Matisse, Marquet, Lehmann, Bussy, Évenepoel, Manguin, Piot, Baignères, and others. All of them benefit from the liberal and intelligent teaching of this maestro.

1893   He presents a work (*Samson Making the Mill Wheel Turn*) for the Rome Prize, but he is unsuccessful.

1894   July. He wins the Chenavard Prize with *The Child Jesus among the Doctors*.

1895   His second attempt to obtain the Rome Prize (with *The Holy Women Mourn for Jesus*) is also unsuccessful. Gustave Moreau, of whom he is the favourite student, advises him to leave the École des Beaux-Arts.

1895-1901 With the exception of 1897 and 1898, he exhibits at the Salon des Artistes Français with oil paintings inspired by the Holy Scriptures such as: *The Child Jesus among the Doctors* (1894), *The Holy Women Mourn for Jesus* (1895), *Jesus and the Disciples of Emaus* (1899), *Salome* (1900) and *Jesus and Judas*. He also paints much from nature and produces landscapes in which his personality is strongly affirmed.

1898   April 18. Gustave Moreau dies. Five years later, Rouault is appointed curator of the museum constituted by the collections which the maestro has left to the French State.

1901   He visits the Abbey of Ligugé with his studio companion Bourbon and there meets Huysmans.

1902-1903 For health reasons he spends two seasons in the Haute Savoie (the second in Évian). With this cure of solitude his vision is renewed.

1902   He devises a new concept of painting which he will practice until approximately 1914. He paints few works in oil on canvas. On the other hand, he paints many watercolors and gouaches on paper, whose characteristics are a synthetic outline and a color range dominated by dark blue. His favourite themes are girls, clowns and characters from the Commedia dell'Arte. The expressive intensity of his figures, together with a fiery lyricism, make Rouault the first of the expressionist painters.

1903-1908 He exhibits frequently at the Salon d'Automne, of which he is one of the founders.

1904   March. He meets Léon Bloy, who later becomes his close friend.

1905-1912 He exhibits regularly at the Salon des Indépendants.

1906   He exhibits at the Berthe Weil Gallery.
He meets Methey, for whom he will decorate numerous ceramic objects (1906-1912) and in whose studio he will meet Ambroise Vollard in 1907.

1908   January 27. He marries Marthe Le Sidaner (sister of the painter Henri Le Sidaner), by whom he will have four children: Geneviève, Isabelle, Michel and Agnès. He frequents the law courts with his friend Granier, and paints judges and courtroom scenes. He also paints humble personages, farm workers, laborers and a series of "down and outs."

1910   February 25 to March 5. His first one-man exhibition at the Galerie Druet, at no. 20, Rue Royale (121 paintings, 8 sketches, 43 stanniferous ceramic pieces, and 10 varnished clay works).

1912   He resides in Versailles and often meets with Jacques and Raïssa Maritain. He becomes friendly with André Suarès.

1913-1917 Ambroise Vollard, initially interested in Rouault's ceramic pieces, buys the works from his studio.

1914-1936 At the same time as painting, Rouault cultivates engraving, to which he devotes much of his time. Using this technique he produces, among other works, *War and Miserere (1917-1927)*, which in 1948 was to appear under the title *Miserere*. For Vollard he illustrates *Les Réincarnations du Père Ubu* 1928), published in 1932, *Cirque de l'Étoile Filante* (1938) and *Passion* (1935-1936), published in 1939, etc.

1918-1930 He abandons watercolor and gouache to devote himself completely to oil painting, searching with more and more insistence for inspiration in religious themes, especially the Passion of Christ. His palette becomes more varied and complete, his material more abundant and his expression more concentrated and grave.

1919   October 17. The first painting by Rouault (*The Child Jesus among the Doctors*), a work which has never before been shown in a museum and which was acquired by the French State in 1917, is exhibited in the Musée de Colmar.

1920 At the Galerie Licorne, a one-man exhibition for Rouault is organized by Dr. Girardin, one of his principal admirers. Others of his admirers are Marcel Sembat and his wife, Olivier Saincère, Stéphane Piot, Gustave Coquiot, Baignères, Dutilleul, Leclanché, John Quinn, Henri Simon and his wife, Heddy Hahnloser and Louise Hervieu.

1921 Michel Puy publishes the first monograph on Rouault in Éditions de la Novelle Revue Française, collection "Les Nouveaux Peintres Françaises."

1922 One-man exhibition at the Galerie Barbazanges.

1924 From May 22 to the end of this same month, a major retrospective is held at the Galerie Druet (88 paintings and 8 ceramic pieces).
On May 15 Jacques Maritain publishes an important text about Rouault in *La Revue universelle*.

1926 Rouault publishes *Souvenirs intimes*, illustrated with lithographs.
Éditions des Quatre-Chemins publishes a book by Georges Charensol with 39 reproductions of works by Rouault.

1929 For Diaghilev Rouault designs the decor for *The Prodigal Son*, with music by Prokofiev.

1930 The Under-Secretary of State for Fine Arts refuses to acquire a painting by Rouault, destined for the Musée du Luxembourg, whose acquisition has been requested by the commission of this museum.
Rouault produces colored etchings for the *Cirque de l'Étoile Filante*, for which he himself writes the text, and for *Passion* by André Suarès. His first exhibitions outside France: in London (Saint George Gallery), Munich (Galerie Neumann), New York (Brummer Gallery) and Chicago (Art Club).

1930-1939 He paints major canvases in which his habitual themes, clowns, pierrots, judges, religious motifs and biblical scenes are treated with a vigorous and varied chromatism, and a rich and transparent material.

1933 He produces cartoons for tapestries.
The first painting by Rouault (*The Holy Countenance*), donated by Mme Chester Dale, enters the Musée du Luxembourg.

1937 In the exhibition "Les Maîtres de l'Art Indépendant," held at the Petit Palais, he presents 49 paintings, of which about twenty were borrowed from Vollard.

1938 The Museum of Modern Art of New York exhibits his engravings.

1939 July 22. Ambroise Vollard dies.

1940-1948 Rouault paints in oils canvases of reduced size, characterized by a thick and abundant material in which blues are the dominant color. His inspiration is by now serene.

1940 Lionello Venturi publishes in E. Weyhe, New York, the first detailed work on Rouault. (Second edition, revised and corrected, in French, published by Skira, Paris and Geneva, in 1948.)
Rouault suffers the exodus from Paris imposed by the occupation of France. His house and studio in Beaumont-sur-Sarthe are looted by German troops.

1945 Major retrospective in the Museum of Modern Art of New York (161 works in catalog).

Canon Devémy and R. P. Couturier ask for five stained glass windows for the Church of Plateau d'Assy. These are produced in the Hébert-Stevens workshop, which have already been responsible for two windows based on cartoons by Rouault.

1947 Rouault wins the court case which has placed him in conflict with Vollard's heirs since the latter's death. On March 19, the tribunal decide that the painter would continue to be owner of Vollard's works "provided that none of these have been given away of his own free will." In consequence all the unfinished canvases are returned to him. However 119 of these last mentioned are missing, having already been disposed of by Vollard's heirs. On November 5, 1948, in front of the tipstaff, Rouault burns 315 of the returned works. He is to repeat this action in 1956 and 1958. A one-man exhibition at the Galerie des Garets, Rue de Courcelles, Paris.
Stella Vespertina is published by René Drouin.

1948 France sends 26 paintings and 12 engravings by Rouault to the Biennial in Venice.
The largest retrospective of works by Rouault takes place in the Kunsthaus in Zurich (263 works in catalog).
He travels to Switzerland and, for the first time, to Italy.
Miserere is exhibited for the first time (Galerie des Garets, Paris).

1948-1952 He works on a series of paintings with colors based on green, yellow and red, and completely renews his palette, nevertheless remaining faithful to his inspiration and love of matter.

1949 He gives his first models for the enamel pieces to be carried out by the workshop in the Abbey of Ligugé.

1951 June 6. On his reaching eighty, the Centre Catholique des Intellectuels Françaises organizes a "Homage to Rouault" in the Palais de Chaillot which constitutes an apotheosis. During this celebration a film about *Miserere*, made under the direction of Abbot Morel, is shown for the first time.

1952 Retrospective in the Palais des Beaux-Arts in Brussels, in the Stedelijk Museum in Amsterdam and the Musée National d'Art Moderne in Paris.

1953 Retrospective in the Cleveland Museum of Art, in the Museum of Modern Art of New York and in the County Museum of Los Angeles.
Retrospective in the National Museum, Tokyo and in Osaka.

1954 Retrospective in the Galleria d'Art Moderna, Milan.

1956 Exhibition in the Musée Toulouse-Lautrec in Albi.

1958 February 13. Georges Rouault dies. The exequies take place on February 17 in the church of Saint-Germain-des-Prés. Following the religious ceremony, in which Abbot Morel speaks, the minister of national education, Billères, and André Lothe, both give a speech in the Place de Saint-Germain-des-Prés.

1963 The widow of Georges Rouault and his children offer a great number of the Maestro's unfinished works to the State of France.

General bibliography

Major writings by Georges Rouault

Souvenirs intimes. Frapier, Paris, 1926.

Cirque de l'Étoile Filante. Verve, Paris, 1943.

Divertissement. Verve, Paris, 1943.

Soliloques. Ides et Calendes, Neuchâtel, 1944.

Stella Vespertina, René Drouin, Paris, 1947.

Correspondances Rouault-Suarès. Gallimard, Paris, 1960. Tokyo, 1971. Stocknell, London, 1983 (extract).

Sur l'art et sur la vie. Denoël et Gonthier, Paris. Società Editrice Internazionale, 1972.

Major books illustrated by Georges Rouault

Petite banlieue. Les Quatre Chemins, Paris, 1929.

Paysages Légendaires. Porteret, Paris, 1929.

Les Réincarnations du Père Ubu. Ambroise Vollard, Paris, 1932.

Cirque de l'Étoile Filante. Ambroise Vollard, Paris, 1932.

Passion. Ambroise Vollard, Paris, 1939.

Stella vespertina. René Drouin, Paris, 1947. (Prologue by Abbot Maurice Morel.)

Miserere. L'Étoile Filante, Paris, 1948. (Reproductions in reduced format from the original edition were published in Paris, 1951; New York, 1952; Tokyo and London, 1963; Assisi, 1966; Dublin and Tokyo, 1971; Seoul, 1978; Milan, 1984; and Paris, 1991.)

Fourteen plate engravings for *Les Fleurs du Mal*. L'Étoile Filante, Paris, 1966.

Visages. Daniel Jacomet et L'Étoile Filante, Paris, 1969. (Foreword by Pierre Courthion.)

Major works on Georges Rouault

Michel Puy, *Georges Rouault*. Nouvelle Revue Française, Paris, 1921.

Georges Charensol, *Georges Rouault, l'homme et l'oeuvre*. Paris, 1962.

Lionello Venturi, *Georges Rouault*. Weyhe, New York, 1940.

Le Point, no. 26-27, *Georges Rouault*. Souillac, 1943.

James Thrall Soby, *Georges Rouault*. Museum of Modern Art, New York, 1945.

Marcel Brion, *Georges Rouault*. Braun, Paris, 1950-1955.

Jacques Lassaigne, *Georges Rouault*. Skira, Geneva, 1951.

Jacques Maritain, *Georges Rouault*. New York, 1953.

Bernard Dorival, *Cinq études sur Georges Rouault*. Éd. Universitaires, Paris, 1956. Bijutsu Shuppan-Sha, Tokyo, 1961.

Claude Roulet, *Rouault, souvenirs*. La Bibliothèque des Arts, Neuchâtel, 1961.

F. Zverina, *Georges Rouault*. Prague, 1961.

Pierre Courthion, *Georges Rouault*. Flammarion, Paris, 1962; Misuzu Shobo, Tokyo, 1962; Il Saggiotare, Milan, 1964; Abrams, New York, 1977; Dumont, Cologne, 1980.

Giuseppe Marchiori, *Georges Rouault*. Silvana, Milan, 1965.

Pierre Courthion, *Rouault*. Nouvelles Éditions Françaises, Paris, 1971.

Waldemar George, Geneviève Nouaille-Rouault, *L'univers de Rouault*. Screpel, Paris, 1971; New York, 1971; Weber, Cologne, 1971; Pall Mall Press, London, 1971.

XXe siècle, special issue, *"Hommage à Rouault,"* Paris, 1971.

Munemoto Yanagi, *Georges Rouault*. Zauho Press, Tokyo, 1972.

Pierre Courthion, Bernard Dorival, Abbot Maurice Morel, *La Passion du Christ*. Iwanami Shoten, Tokyo, 1975.

Bernard Dorival, *Rouault*, Shinchosha, Tokyo, 1976.

Nora Possenti Ghiglia and others, *Rouault*. Bagaloni, Ancona, 1977.

François Chapon, Isabelle Rouault, *Rouault Œuvre gravé*. Montecarlo, 1978. (Text in French, English and German.) Iwanami Shoten, Tokyo, 1979.

Geneviève Nouaille-Rouault, H. Takata, *Rouault*. The Book of Great Masters, Tokyo, Zauho Press, Shogakukan, 1979.

Bernard Dorival, *Rouault*. Flammarion, Paris, 1982, Bonfini Press Corporation, Naefels, 1983; Easton Press, Norwalk, 1984.

Danielle Molinari, *Rouault*, Musée de la Ville de Paris, Paris, 1983. (Catalog raisonné of the works in the museum collection.)

Rainer Beck, Siegfried Gohr, *Georges Rouault*. Joseph Haubrich Kunsthalle, Cologne, 1983.

Yanagi Munemoto, *Georges Rouault, peintre de l'âme chrétienne*. Gakken, Tokyo, 1987.

Carmine Benincasa, *G. Rouault*. Edizioni Seat, Turin, 1988.

Curt Grützmacher and others, *Georges Rouault*. Kunstamt Wedding, Berlin, 1988.

Bernard Dorival, Isabelle Rouault, *L'Œuvre peint*, Catalog raisonné. André Sauret, Montecarlo, 1988; Iwanami, Tokyo, 1990. (Text in French and English.)

ILLUSTRATIONS

Due to lack of reliable information, the support used by the artist for his works is not always mentioned, although it seems that Rouault usually painted on paper which he subsequently pasted onto canvas.
For reasons of discretion, the names of the private collections are not included.

1. Study for *Samson Making the Mill Wheel Turn*. 1893.
   India ink pen drawing, 8¼×4½ in. (21×11.5 cm).
   Los Angeles County Funds, Los Angeles.

2. Study for *The Child Jesus among the Doctors*. 1894.
   Pen drawing, 6¼×5⅜ in. (16×13.5 cm).

3. *The Child Jesus among the Doctors*. 1894.
   Oil, 57½×44⅞ in. (146×114 cm).
   Musée des Unterlinden, Colmar.

1

2

3

4. *Nighttime Landscape (The Brawl in the Works).* 1897.
   Watercolor and pastel, 24¾×33½ in. (63×85 cm).
   Musée d'Orsay, Paris.

4

5. *Bathers*. 1903.
   Watercolor, 17⅜×13 in. (44×33 cm).

6. *The Holy Countenance*. 1904.
   Tempera and gouache (highlighted with gilt dust), 20⅛×15⅜ in. (51×39 cm).

6

7. *The Poulots*, also known as *The Couple, Red Zone (a Study of Habits)*. 1905.
   Watercolor, 27⅝×20½ in. (70×52 cm).

8. *The Expert Horsewoman (The Female Clown)*. 1906.
Watercolor and pastel, 27 × 20½ in. (68.5×52 cm).
Musée d'Art Moderne de la Ville de Paris.

9. *In Tabarin (The Uproar).* 1905.
   Watercolor and pastel, 28 × 21⅝ in. (71×55 cm).
   Musée d'Art Moderne de la Ville de Paris.

10. *Women in the Café*. 1906.
Watercolor, 8⅝×6¾ in. (22×17 cm).

10

11. *Girl with Mirror*. 1906.
Watercolor, 28⅜×21⅝ in. (72×55 cm).
Musée National d'Art Moderne. Centre Georges-Pompidou, Paris.

12

13

12. *Heads in Massacre (Marionettes and the "Mariée")*. 1907.
Oil, 29½×41¾ in. (75×106 cm).
The Tate Gallery, London.

13. *Odalisque*. 1906.
Watercolor and pastel, 21¼×24 in. (54×61 cm).
Museum of Copenhagen.

14. *The Conjurer (Pierrot)*. 1907.
Oil and watercolor, 17⅜×13 in. (44×33 cm).

15. *Nude with Arms Upraised (Combing her Hair)*. 1907.
Watercolor, pastel, India ink and oil, 11⅞×12 in. (30×30.5 cm).
Musée d'Art Moderne de la Ville de Paris.

15

16. *The Barge*. 1909.
   Mixture of watercolor and gouache, 22½×34⅝ in. (57×88 cm).
   Musée des Beaux-Arts de Grenoble.

17. *Judges*. 1908.
   Oil, 29½×41⅜ in. (75×105 cm).
   Royal Fine Arts Museum of Copenhagen.

16

17

18. *Girls*. Around 1909.
    Oil, 35½×23⅝ in. (90×60 cm).

19. *The Slum of Great Sorrows (Mother and Children)*. 1911.
Paste tempera, India ink and charcoal, 12¼×7¾ in. (31×19.8 cm).
Musée d'Art Moderne de la Ville de Paris.

20. *Country Folk*. 1911.
Oil, 35×24 in. (89×61 cm).

19

20

21. *Winter III*. 1910.
Turpentine paint, pastel and wax crayon, 7⅝×12¼ in. (19.5×31 cm).
Musée d'Art Moderne de la Ville de Paris.

22. *Winter Exodus*. 1911.
Gouache and pastel, 10×16¾ in. (25.5×42.5 cm).

23. *The Fugitives (The Exodus)*. 1911.
   Gouache and pastel, 17¾×24 in. (45×61 cm).
   Kunsthaus, Zurich.

23

24. *The Baptism of Jesus*. 1911.
Watercolor and pastel, 24¾×22⅞ in. (63×58 cm., oval.
Musée d'Art Moderne de la Ville de Paris.

24

25. *White Pierrot*. 1911.
   Watercolor and pastel, 30¾×25⅝ in. (78×65 cm).

26. *The Widow I.* 1912.
   Watercolor, India ink and charcoal, 11⅝×7⅛ in. (29.5×18 cm).
   Musée d'Art Moderne de la Ville de Paris.

27. *Tragic Clown*. Around 1912.
    Oil, 35⅜×26⅞ in. (89.8×68.2 cm).
    Collection The Museum of Modern Art, New York.
    Nate B. and Frances Spingold Donation.

28. *Acrobat I (Fighter)*. Around 1913.
    Tempera, 11⅞×7⅜ in. (30.3×19.3 cm).

29. *Acrobat XVI (Fighter)*. Around 1913.
    Oil and gouache, 41×28¾ in. (104×73 cm).

28

30. *Madame X.* 1912-1913.
Tempera, 12⅜×7⅞ in. (31.5×20 cm).
Musée d'Art Moderne de la Ville de Paris.

31. *The Poser (Super Man).* 1912-1913.
Paste tempera, watercolor and charcoal, 12¼×7⅛ in.
(31×18 cm).
Musée d'Art Moderne de la Ville de Paris.

32. *La Belle Hélène* (sketch). 1910-1919.
India ink wash, paste tempera and pastel, 12¼×7½ in.
(31×19 cm).
Musée d'Art Moderne de la Ville de Paris.

33. *The Prude.* 1910-1919.
Small format.

30

31

32

33

34. *Nudes*. 1914.
    Composition. Gouache or paste tempera, 19⅞×13⅜ in. (50.5×34 cm).
    National Gallery of Prague.

34

35. *Ecce Homo*. 1914.
   Oil and tempera, 20⅞×13⅜ in. (53×34 cm).

36. *Judges*. 1914.
   Oil, 21½×14¾ in. (54.5×37.5 cm).

35

36

37. *Jesus Christ on the Cross*. 1914.
    Gouache and oil, 18⅞×13¾ in. (48×35 cm).

38

39

38. *The Super Man*. 1916.
    Oil, 41¾×29½ in. (106×75 cm).

39. *In the Hostel*. 1914.
    Gouache or tempera, 21¼×28⅜ in. (54×72 cm).
    National Gallery of Prague.

40. *Landscape with Large Trees*. 1915.
    Oil, 30¾×22⅜ in. (78×57.5 cm).

41. *Arabesque (Two Nudes)*. 1917.
    Watercolor, 15⅜×10 in. (39×25.5 cm).

42. *The Good Negro (for Ubu)*. Around 1918.
    Wash of India ink, 10¼×7¼ in. (26×18.5 cm).

43. *Le Père Ubu*. 1918.
    Watercolor and pencils, 15×9½ in. (38×24 cm).

44. *The Professor of the Cask*. 1918.
    Wash of India ink, 10¼×7⅝ in. (26×19.5 cm).

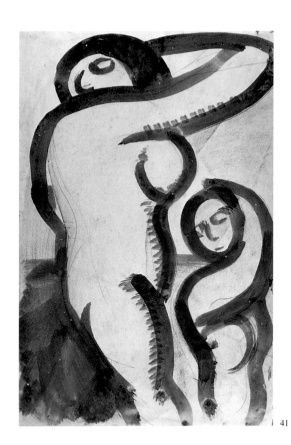

41

42

43

44

45. *Bureaucrat*. 1917.
   Wash and watercolor, 11⅞×6¾ in. 30×17 cm.
   Collection The Museum of Modern Art, New York.
   Abby Aldrich Rockefeller Donation.

46. *Trio (Three Clowns)*. 1917-1920.
Oil, 41⅜×29½ in. (105×75 cm).

47. *The Old Clown*. 1917-1920.
      Oil, 40⅛×29¾ in. (102×75.5 cm).

48. *Jesus on the Cross.* Around 1920.
Oil, 25⅝×19¾ / 20½×15¾ in. (65×50 / 52×40 cm).

49. *Jesus in the Slums*. 1920-1924.
    Oil, 36¼×29⅛ in. (92×74 cm).
    Bridgestone Museum, Tokyo.

50. *The Old Clown with his Dog*. Around 1925.
Oil, 28¾×18⅞ in. (73×48 cm).
Kiyoharu Museum, Shirakaba, Japan.

51. *The Little Horsewoman*. Around 1925.
Oil, 19½×22⅞ in. (49.5×58 cm).
Idemitsu Museum, Tokyo.

52. *Circus Horsewoman*. Around 1926.
Oil, 28⅜×20⅛ in. (72×51 cm).
Bridgestone Museum, Tokyo.

51

52

53. *Feminine Nude*. Around 1925.
Oil, 21½×23⅜ in. (80×60 cm).

54. *The Apprentice Craftsman (Self-Portrait)*. Around 1925.
   Oil, 26×20½ in. (66×52 cm).
   Musée National d'Art Moderne. Centre Georges-Pompidou, Paris.

55. *Who Does not Make Up?*
    Plate 8 of *Miserere*, 1917-1927.

56. *Bella Matribus Detestata.*
    Plate 42 of *Miserere*. 1917-1927.

57. *In so many Diverse Orders, the Beautiful Task of Sowing Barren Land.*
    Plate 22 of *Miserere*. 1917-1927.

58. *Sunt Lacrymae Rerum . . .*
    Plate 27 of *Miserere*, 1917-1927.

Qui ne se grime pas?

55

Bella matribus detestata.

56

En tant d'ordres divers, le beau métier
d'ensemencer une terre hostile.

57

Sunt lacrymæ rerum...

58

59. *Believing Ourselves Kings.*
    Plate 7 of *Miserere*, 1917-1927.

60. *Lady of High Lineage Believes She Has a Place Reserved in Heaven.*
    Plate 16 of *Miserere*, 1917-1927.

61. *In a Mouth that was Fresh, the Taste of Bile.*
    Plate 15 of *Miserere*, 1917-1927.

62. *The Hard Task of Living . . .*
    Plate 12 of *Miserere*, 1917-1927.

nous croyant rois.

59

Dame du Haut-Quartier croit prendre
pour le Ciel place réservée.

60

En bouche qui fut fraîche, goût de fiel.

61

Le dur métier de vivre...

62

63. *"Jesus Shall Remain in Agony until the End of the World. . ."*
Plate 35 of *Miserere*, 1917-1927.

64. *Lord, if it is You, I Recognize You.*
Plate 32 of *Miserere*, 1917-1927.

65. *Dura Lex Sed Lex.*
Plate 52 of *Miserere*, 1917-1927.

66. *The Blind Man Sometimes Comforts He Who Sees.*
Plate 55 of *Miserere*, 1917-1927.

"Jésus sera en agonie jusqu'à la fin du monde..."

63

Seigneur, c'est vous, je vous reconnais.

64

Dura lex sed lex.

65

L'aveugle parfois a consolé le voyant.

66

67. *"Long Live the Dead!"*
Plate 54 of *Miserere*, 1917-1927.

68. *This Will Be the Last, Minimal Father!*
Plate 36 of *Miserere*, 1917-1927.

69. *De Profundis. . .*
Plate 47 of *Miserere*, 1917-1927.

70. *"The Just Man, like Sandalwood, Perfumes the Axe that Strikes Him."*
Plate 46 of *Miserere*, 1917-1927.

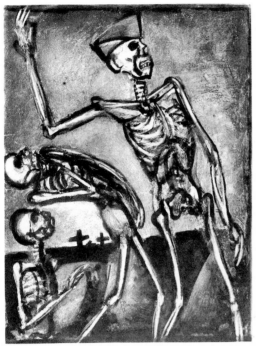

"Debout les morts!"

67

Ce sera la dernière, petit père!

68

De profundis...

69

"Le juste, comme le bois de santal,
parfume la hache qui le frappe"

70

71

72

71. *Self-Portrait*. 1925.
    Lithographic pencil, 8¼×6½ in. (21×16.5 cm).

72. "*. . . To the Poor Man or the Orphan . . .*" 1929.
    Gouache applied to a photograph, Small format.

73. *Who Does not Make Up?* After 1930.
    Oil and gouache. Medium-size format.
    Indianapolis Museum of Art.

74. *"... When Night Fell, the Moon Came Out."* 1930.
11⅞×18⅞× in. 30×48 cm).
Museum of Antwerp.

75. *Twilight (Sea Shore)*. 1939.
Oil, 19¾×25⅝ in. (50.1×65.1 cm).
The Phillips Collection, Washington.

76. *Tragic*. 1930.
India ink, pastel and gouache, 19×11⅝ in. (48.3×29.5 cm).

74

75

77

78

77. *Clowns and Ballerina*. 1933.
Oil, 26¼×19¾ in. (66.5×50 cm).

78. *"Three Clowns."* 1931.
Gouache, 7⅛×9⅞ in. (18×25 cm).

79. *The Wounded Clown I*. 1932.
Oil, 78¾×47¼ in. (200×120 cm).
Musée National d'Art Moderne.
Centre Georges-Pompidou, Paris.

80

81

80. *"Apparition" (Jesus Christ Emerging from the Tomb)*. 1935-1936.
    Oil, 17¾×13 / 12¼×8¼ in. (44×33 / 31×21 cm).

81. *The Holy Countenance*. 1933.
    Oil, 35⅞×25⅝ in. (91×65 cm).
    Musée National d'Art Moderne. Centre Georges-Pompidou, Paris.

82. *Jesus Christ Abused*. Around 1932.
    36¼×28½ in. (92×72.4 cm).
    Collection The Museum of Modern Art, New York. Anonymous Donation.

83. *"The Wandering Jew."* 1932 or 1934.
    Gouache, 7⅞×10⅝ / 7¼×10⅞ in. (20×27 / 18.5×27.6 cm).

84. *"Passion." Jesus Christ "Ecce Dolor."* 1935-1936.
    Oil, 13⅝×11 / 9×8⅛ in. (34.5×28 / 23×20.5 cm).

85. *"Via Crucis IV."* 1935-1936.
    Oil, 13×12¾ / 6¾×8⅝ in. (33×32.5 / 17×22 cm).

86. *Pierrot and Small Ballerina.* 1934.
    Oil, 12⅜×7⅞ in. (31.5×20 cm).

83

84

85

87

88

89

87. *"... This Deserted Street Bordered by Two Palaces."* 1935-1936.
Oil, 17⅜×13 / 11⅞×7⅞ in. (44×33 / 30×20 cm).
Idemitsu Museum, Tokyo.

88. *"The Olive Grove."* 1935-1936.
Oil, 17⅜×13 / 11⅞×7⅞ in. (44×33 / 30×20 cm).
Idemitsu Museum, Tokyo.

89. *Jesus with the Fishermen.* 1937.
Oil, 27×50¼ in. (68.5×127.5 cm).
Musée de l'Art Moderne de la Ville de Paris.

90

91

92

93

90. *"The Man with Myrrh."* 1936.
Oil, 17⅜×13 / 11⅞×7⅞ in. (44×33 / 30×20 cm).
Idemitsu Museum, Tokyo.

91. *"What Furrows for Blood, What Labor for Tears."*
1935-1936.
Oil, 17⅜×13 / 11⅞×7⅞ in. (44×33 / 30×20 cm).
Idemitsu Museum, Tokyo.

92. *"Here Is the Man."* 1935-1936.
Oil, 17⅜×13 / 7⅞×11⅞ in. (44×33 / 20×30 cm).
Idemitsu Museum, Tokyo.

93. *"Here a World Becomes Hidden and Dies: Another World is Born."*
1935-1936.
Oil, 17⅜×13 / 4×7⅞ in. (44×33 / 10×20 cm).
Idemitsu Museum, Tokyo.

94. *The Old King.* 1937.
Oil, 29½×20⅞ in. (75×53 cm).
Carnegie Institute, Pittsburgh.

94

95

96

95. *Pierrot*. 1937-1938.
    Oil, 21⅞×18⅛ in. (55.5×46 cm).

96. *Leaning Nude*. 1937 or 1938.
    Oil, 8¼×7⅛ in. (21×18 cm).

97. *Bust of Woman*. 1939.
    Oil, 21¼×16½ in. (54×42 cm).

97

98. *The Flight to Egypt*. 1938.
16⅜×10⅜ in. (41.5×27 cm).
Musée d'Art Moderne de la Ville de Paris.

99. *Jesus with Children (Slums)*. 1931-1939.
Oil, 11⅞×8⅞ in. (30×22.5 cm).

100. *Sunset*. 1937-1939.
31¼×23½ in. (79.4×59.7 cm).
The Solomon R. Guggenheim Museum, New York.

101. *Jesus Christ (and Pharisees)*. 1938.
Oil, 29⅛×41⅜ in. (74×105 cm).
Idemitsu Museum, Tokyo.

98

99

100

101

102. *Jesus Christ*. 1937 or 1938.
    Oil, 26⅜×18⅞ in. (67×48 cm).

103. *"Jesus Christ" (Passion)*. 1937.
   Oil, 41⅜×29½ in. (105×75 cm).
   The Cleveland Museum of Art. Donation by the Hanna Foundation.

104

104. *Bunch of Flowers in Yellow Vase*. 1939.
Oil, 13¾×9⅞ in. (34.9×25 cm).
The Phillips Collection, Washington.

105. *Autumn*. 1938.
Oil, 26¾×40⅛ in. (68×102 cm).

106. *Twilight (Île de France)*. 1937.
Oil, 40×28½ in. (101.5×72.5 cm).

105

107. *Profile of Woman.* 1939.
Oil, 25¼×19¼ in. (64×49 cm).
The Art Institute of Chicago.

108. *Decorative Flowers*. 1939.
    Oil, 17½×13 in. (44.5×33 cm).

109. *Jesus at the Lake of Tiberiades*. 1939.
Oil, 13¼×20½ in. (33.5×52 cm).

110. *Biblical Landscape*. 1939.
Oil, 20¼×28¾ in. (51.5×73 cm).

109

110

111. *Fishing Boats with Sunset.* 1939.
Oil, 17¾×25¼ in. (45×64 cm).

112. *Judges*. 1939.
     Oil, 10⅞×8½ / 10½×8¼ in. (27.5×21.5 / 27×21 cm).

112

113. *Blue Pierrots*. Around 1943.
Oil, 23¼×17¾ in. (59×45 cm).

114

114. *Biblical Landscape*. Around 1945.
Oil, 9⅞×11⅜ in. (25×29 cm).

115. *Christian Intimacy (Jesus with Martha and Mary)*. Around 1945.
18⅛×25⅝ in. (46×65 cm).

116. *Veronica*. Around 1945.
Oil, 19¾×14⅛ in. (50×36 cm).
Musée National d'Art Moderne. Centre Georges-Pompidou, Paris.

115

117. *The Flight to Egypt.* 1945-1946.
Oil, 24 × 18½ in. (61×47 cm).

118. *Jacob's Well*. 1945-1946.
     Oil, 12⅝×19⅞ in. (32×50.5 cm).

119. *De Profundis*. Around 1946.
Oil, 26¼×20⅛ in. (66.5×51 cm).
Musée National d'Art Moderne. Centre Georges-Pompidou, Paris.

120. *The Holy Countenance*. Around 1946.
19¾×14⅛ in. (50×36 cm).
Museum of the Vatican.

121

122

123

121. *The Guardian Angel*. 1946.
Gouache, 11⅜×8¼ in. (29×21 cm).

122. *On the Banks of the Jordan*. Around 1947.
Oil, 17⅜×13⅜ in. (44×34 cm).
Musée de Dijon.

123. *Biblical Landscape*. 1946.
Oil, 14⅜×20⅛ in. (36.5×51 cm).

124. *The Road to Nazareth*. 1946.
Oil, 19¾×14⅛ in. (50×36 cm).
Museum of Ghent.

125. *The Sybil of Cumas*. 1947.
Oil, 20½×14⅝ in. (52×37 cm).

126. *Carmencita II*. 1947.
Oil, 19¼×12¼ in. (49×31 cm).

127. *Teresina*. 1947.
Oil, 20⅛×13¾ in. (51×35 cm).

126

127

128

128. *Visionary*. 1946.
Oil, 13½×10½ in. (34.3×26.7 cm).
Musée National d'Art Moderne.
Centre Georges-Pompidou, Paris.

129. *Decorative Flowers*. 1947.
Oil, 22½×15⅜ in. (57×39 cm).

130. *"Homo Homini Lupus."* 1944-1948.
Oil, 25¼×18⅛ in. (64×46 cm).
Musée National d'Art Moderne.
Centre Georges-Pompidou, Paris.

129

131. *Pedro*. Around 1948.
    Oil, 26 × 17¾ in. (66×45 cm).

132. *Duo (The Two Brothers)*. Around 1948.
    Oil, 25¼×16½ in. (64×42 cm).
    Musée National d'Art Moderne. Centre Georges-Pompidou, Paris.

131

132

133. *Pierrot*. Around 1948.
     Oil, 21¼×15 in. (54×38 cm).

134. *Autumn (Nazareth)*. 1948.
Oil, 26¾×41⅜ in. (68×105 cm).
Museum of the Vatican.

135. *Old Slum (Mother and Children)*. 1951.
Oil, 10¼×8¼ in. (26×21 cm).

136. *Old Slum (St. Joan of Arc)*. 1951.
Oil, 11⅞×9½ in. (30×24 cm).

134

135

136

137. *Autumn Nocturne.* 1952.
Oil, 29½×39⅜ in. (75×100 cm).

137

138. *End of Autumn III*. 1952.
Oil, 41×29⅛ in. (104×74 cm).

139

140

139. *Still Life with Oranges*. 1953.
    Oil, 13⅜×18½ in. (34×47 cm).

140. *Decorative Flowers*. Around 1953.
    Oil, 37×25¼ in. (94×64 cm).

141. *Sara*. 1956.
    Oil, 21⅝×16½ in. (55×42 cm).
    Studio of G. Rouault.

141

List of illustrations

44. *The Professor of the Cask*. 1918.
Wash of India ink, 10¼×7⅝ in.
(26×19.5 cm).

45. *Bureaucrat*. 1917.
Wash and watercolor, 11⅞×6¾ in.
30×17 cm.
Collection The Museum of Modern Art, New York.
Abby Aldrich Rockefeller Donation.

46. *Trio (Three Clowns)*. 1917-1920.
Oil, 41⅜×29½ in. (105×75 cm).

47. *The Old Clown*. 1917-1920.
Oil, 40⅛×29¾ in. (102×75.5 cm).

48. *Jesus on the Cross*. Around 1920.
Oil, 25⅝×19¾ / 20½×15¾ in.
(65×50 / 52×40 cm).

49. *Jesus in the Slums*. 1920-1924.
Oil, 36¼×29⅛ in. (92×74 cm).
Bridgestone Museum, Tokyo.

50. *The Old Clown with his Dog*. Around 1925.
Oil, 28¾×18⅞ in. (73×48 cm).
Kiyoharu Museum, Shirakaba, Japan.

51. *The Little Horsewoman*. Around 1925.
Oil, 19½×22⅞ in. (49.5×58 cm).
Idemitsu Museum, Tokyo.

52. *Circus Horsewoman*. Around 1926.
Oil, 28⅜×20⅛ in. (72×51 cm).
Bridgestone Museum, Tokyo.

53. *Feminine Nude*. Around 1925.
Oil, 21½×23⅝ in. (80×60 cm).

54. *The Apprentice Craftsman (Self-Portrait)*. Around 1925.
Oil, 26×20½ in. (66×52 cm).
Musée National d'Art Moderne.
Centre Georges-Pompidou, Paris.

55. *Who Does not Make Up?*
Plate 8 of *Miserere*, 1917-1927.

56. *Bella Matribus Detestata*.
Plate 42 of *Miserere*. 1917-1927.

57. *In so many Diverse Orders, the Beautiful Task of Sowing Barren Land*.
Plate 22 of *Miserere*. 1917-1927.

58. *Sunt Lacrymae Rerum . . .*
Plate 27 of *Miserere*, 1917-1927.

59. *Believing Ourselves Kings*.
Plate 7 of *Miserere*, 1917-1927.

60. *Lady of High Lineage Believes She Has a Place Reserved in Heaven*.
Plate 16 of *Miserere*, 1917-1927.

61. *In a Mouth that was Fresh, the Taste of Bile*.
Plate 15 of *Miserere*, 1917-1927.

62. *The Hard Task of Living . . .*
Plate 12 of *Miserere*, 1917-1927.

63. *"Jesus Shall Remain in Agony until the End of the World. . ."*
Plate 35 of *Miserere*, 1917-1927.

64. *Lord, if it is You, I Recognize You*.
Plate 32 of *Miserere*, 1917-1927.

65. *Dura Lex Sed Lex*.
Plate 52 of *Miserere*, 1917-1927.

66. *The Blind Man Sometimes Comforts He Who Sees*.
Plate 55 of *Miserere*, 1917-1927.

67. *"Long Live the Dead!"*
Plate 54 of *Miserere*, 1917-1927.

68. *This Will Be the Last, Minimal Father!*
Plate 36 of *Miserere*, 1917-1927.

69. *De Profundis. . .*
Plate 47 of *Miserere*, 1917-1927.

70. *"The Just Man, like Sandalwood, Perfumes the Axe that Strikes Him."*
Plate 46 of *Miserere*, 1917-1927.

71. *Self-Portrait*. 1925.
Lithographic pencil, 8¼×6½ in.
(21×16.5 cm).

72. *". . . To the Poor Man or the Orphan . . ."* 1929.
Gouache applied to a photograph,
Small format.

73. *Who Does not Make Up?* After 1930.
Oil and gouache.
Medium-size format.
Indianapolis Museum of Art.

74. *". . . When Night Fell, the Moon Came Out."* 1930.
11⅞×18⅞× in. 30×48 cm).
Museum of Antwerp.

75. *Twilight (Sea Shore)*. 1939.
Oil, 19¾×25⅝ in. (50.1×65.1 cm).
The Phillips Collection, Washington.

76. *Tragic*. 1930.
India ink, pastel and gouache, 19×11⅝ in. (48.3×29.5 cm).

77. *Clowns and Ballerina*. 1933.
Oil, 26¼×19¾ in. (66.5×50 cm).

78. *"Three Clowns."* 1931.
Gouache, 7⅛×9⅞ in. (18×25 cm).

79. *The Wounded Clown I*. 1932.
Oil, 78¾×47¼ in. (200×120 cm).
Musée National d'Art Moderne.
Centre Georges-Pompidou, Paris.

80. *"Apparition" (Jesus Christ Emerging from the Tomb)*. 1935-1936.
Oil, 17¾×13 / 12¼×8¼ in.
(44×33 / 31×21 cm).

81. *The Holy Countenance*. 1933.
Oil, 35⅞×25⅝ in. (91×65 cm).
Musée National d'Art Moderne.
Centre Georges-Pompidou, Paris.

82. *Jesus Christ Abused*. Around 1932.
36¼×28½ in. (92×72.4 cm).
Collection The Museum of Modern Art, New York.
Anonymous Donation.

83. *"The Wandering Jew."* 1932 or 1934.
Gouache, 7⅞×10⅝ / 7¼×10⅞ in.
(20×27 / 18.5×27.6 cm).

84. *"Passion." Jesus Christ "Ecce Dolor."* 1935-1936.
Oil, 13⅝×11 / 9×8⅛ in.
(34.5×28 / 23×20.5 cm).

85. *"Via Crucis IV."* 1935-1936.
Oil, 13×12¾ / 6¾×8⅝ in. (33×32.5 / 17×22 cm).

86. *Pierrot and Small Ballerina*. 1934.
Oil, 12⅜×7⅞ in. (31.5×20 cm).

87. *". . . This Deserted Street Bordered by Two Palaces."* 1935-1936.
Oil, 17⅜×13 / 11⅞×7⅞ in.
(44×33 / 30×20 cm).
Idemitsu Museum, Tokyo.

88. *"The Olive Grove."* 1935-1936.
Oil, 17⅜×13 / 11⅞×7⅞ in.
(44×33 / 30×20 cm).
Idemitsu Museum, Tokyo.

89. *Jesus with the Fishermen*. 1937.
Oil, 27×50¼ in. (68.5×127.5 cm).
Musée de l'Art Moderne de la Ville de Paris.

90. *"The Man with Myrrh."* 1936.
Oil, 17⅜×13 / 11⅞×7⅞ in.
(44×33 / 30×20 cm).
Idemitsu Museum, Tokyo.

91. *"What Furrows for Blood, What Labor for Tears."* 1935-1936.
Oil, 17⅜×13 / 11⅞×7⅞ in.
(44×33 / 30×20 cm).
Idemitsu Museum, Tokyo.

92. *"Here Is the Man."* 1935-1936.
Oil, 17⅜×13 / 7⅞×11⅞ in.
(44×33 / 20×30 cm).
Idemitsu Museum, Tokyo.

93. *"Here a World Becomes Hidden and Dies: Another World is Born."* 1935-1936.
Oil, 17⅜×13 / 4×7⅞ in.
(44×33 / 10×20 cm).
Idemitsu Museum, Tokyo.

94. *The Old King*. 1937.
Oil, 29½×20⅞ in. (75×53 cm).
Carnegie Institute, Pittsburgh.

95. *Pierrot*. 1937-1938.
Oil, 21⅞×18⅛ in. (55.5×46 cm).

96. *Leaning Nude*. 1937 or 1938.
Oil, 8¼×7⅛ in. (21×18 cm).

97. *Bust of Woman*. 1939.
Oil, 21¼×16½ in. (54×42 cm).

98. *The Flight to Egypt*. 1938.
16⅜×10⅝ in. (41.5×27 cm).
Musée d'Art Moderne de la Ville de Paris.

99. *Jesus with Children (Slums)*. 1931-1939.
Oil, 11⅞×8⅞ in. (30×22.5 cm).

100. *Sunset*. 1937-1939.
31¼×23½ in. (79.4×59.7 cm).
The Solomon R. Guggenheim Museum, New York.

101. *Jesus Christ (and Pharisees)*. 1938.
Oil, 29⅛×41⅜ in. (74×105 cm).
Idemitsu Museum, Tokyo.

102. *Jesus Christ*. 1937 or 1938.
Oil, 26⅜×18⅞ in. (67×48 cm).

103. *"Jesus Christ" (Passion)*. 1937.
Oil, 41⅜×29½ in. (105×75 cm).
The Cleveland Museum of Art.
Donation by the Hanna Foundation.

104. *Bunch of Flowers in Yellow Vase*. 1939.
Oil, 13¾×9⅞ in. (34.9×25 cm).
The Phillips Collection, Washington.

105. *Autumn*. 1938.
Oil, 26¾×40⅛ in. (68×102 cm).

106. *Twilight (Île de France)*. 1937.
Oil, 40×28½ in. (101.5×72.5 cm).

107. *Profile of Woman*. 1939.
Oil, 25¼×19¼ in. (64×49 cm).
The Art Institute of Chicago.

108. *Decorative Flowers*. 1939.
Oil, 17½×13 in. (44.5×33 cm).

109. *Jesus at the Lake of Tiberiades*. 1939.
Oil, 13¼×20½ in. (33.5×52 cm).

110. *Biblical Landscape*. 1939.
Oil, 20¼×28¾ in. (51.5×73 cm).

111. *Fishing Boats with Sunset*. 1939.
Oil, 17¾×25¼ in. (45×64 cm).

112. *Judges*. 1939.
Oil, 10⅞×8½ / 10½×8¼ in.
(27.5×21.5 / 27×21 cm).

113. *Blue Pierrots*. Around 1943.
Oil, 23¼×17¾ in. (59×45 cm).

114. *Biblical Landscape*. Around 1945.
Oil, 9⅞×11⅜ in. (25×29 cm).

115. *Christian Intimacy (Jesus with Martha and Mary)*. Around 1945.
18⅛×25⅝ in. (46×65 cm).

116. *Veronica*. Around 1945.
Oil, 19¾×14⅛ in. (50×36 cm).
Musée National d'Art Moderne.
Centre Georges-Pompidou, Paris.

117. *The Flight to Egypt*. 1945-1946.
Oil, 24×18½ in. (61×47 cm).

118. *Jacob's Well*. 1945-1946.
Oil, 12⅝×19⅞ in. (32×50.5 cm).

119. *De Profundis*. Around 1946.
Oil, 26¼×20⅛ in. (66.5×51 cm).
Musée National d'Art Moderne.
Centre Georges-Pompidou, Paris.

120. *The Holy Countenance*. Around 1946.
19¾×14⅛ in. (50×36 cm).
Museum of the Vatican.

121. *The Guardian Angel*. 1946.
Gouache, 11⅜×8¼ in. (29×21 cm).

122. *On the Banks of the Jordan*. Around 1947.
Oil, 17⅜×13⅜ in. (44×34 cm).
Musée de Dijon.

123. *Biblical Landscape*. 1946.
Oil, 14⅜×20⅛ in. (36.5×51 cm).

124. *The Road to Nazareth*. 1946.
Oil, 19¾×14⅛ in. (50×36 cm).
Museum of Ghent.

125. *The Sybil of Cumas*. 1947.
Oil, 20½×14⅝ in. (52×37 cm).

126. *Carmencita II*. 1947.
Oil, 19¼×12¼ in. (49×31 cm).

127. *Teresina*. 1947.
Oil, 20⅛×13¾ in. (51×35 cm).

128. *Visionary*. 1946.
Oil, 13½×10½ in. (34.3×26.7 cm).
Musée National d'Art Moderne.
Centre Georges-Pompidou, Paris.

129. *Decorative Flowers*. 1947.
Oil, 22½×15⅜ in. (57×39 cm).

130. *"Homo Homini Lupus."* 1944-1948.
Oil, 25¼×18⅛ in. (64×46 cm).
Musée National d'Art Moderne.
Centre Georges-Pompidou, Paris.

131. *Pedro*. Around 1948.
Oil, 26×17¾ in. (66×45 cm).

132. *Duo (The Two Brothers)*. Around 1948.
Oil, 25¼×16½ in. (64×42 cm).
Musée National d'Art Moderne.
Centre Georges-Pompidou, Paris.

133. *Pierrot*. Around 1948.
Oil, 21¼×15 in. (54×38 cm).

134. *Autumn (Nazareth)*. 1948.
Oil, 26¾×41⅜ in. (68×105 cm).
Museum of the Vatican.

135. *Old Slum (Mother and Children)*. 1951.
Oil, 10¼×8¼ in. (26×21 cm).

136. *Old Slum (St. Joan of Arc)*. 1951.
Oil, 11⅞×9½ in. (30×24 cm).

137. *Autumn Nocturne*. 1952.
Oil, 29½×39⅜ in. (75×100 cm).

138. *End of Autumn III*. 1952.
Oil, 41×29⅛ in. (104×74 cm).

139. *Still Life with Oranges*. 1953.
Oil, 13⅜×18½ in. (34×47 cm).

140. *Decorative Flowers*. Around 1953.
Oil, 37×25¼ in. (94×64 cm).

141. *Sara*. 1956.
Oil, 21⅝×16½ in. (55×42 cm).
Studio of G. Rouault.